ARTE CONCRETO INVENCION
ARTE MADI

ARTE CONCRETO INVENCION
ARTE MADI

EDITION GALERIE VON BARTHA BASEL

The Negation of all Melancholy[1]

Arte Madí/Concreto-Invención 1944–1950

by Gabriel Pérez-Barreiro

With the publication in 1944 of *Arturo* magazine,[2] a fundamentally new attitude became evident in Argentine art, signalling the birth of the first truly Argentine avant-garde movement in the visual arts. From a rather muddled set of intentions set out in *Arturo* a series of movements of geometrical abstraction developed, of which the most significant are the Madí Movement, the Asociatión Arte Concreto-Invención, and Perceptismo. Each of these movements in its own way reflected a growing complexity in the Argentine relationship with European artistic developments. In as much as *Arturo* symbolises a break with existing notions of cultural centrality, the generation of 1944, with all its contradictions, forceful personalities and disputes, is an accurate reflection of the political crisis of modern Argentina. It is in this light that geometrical abstraction in Argentina must be seen: not as a slavish copying of European models but rather as an original reinterpretation of these models, and also a profound meditation on the semantic problems of finding a language with which to express a new set of ambitions, and charging this "universal" language with local concerns.

Argentina in 1944 was facing a major structural crisis, as the descendants of the several waves of immigrants who shaped Buenos Aires from the turn of the century began to demand a political voice in a power structure largely untouched since Independence, and whose aims were particularly frustrated during the political stagnation of the 1930s, the "década infama". Ultimately this crisis resulted in the rise of Peronism, a uniquely Argentine mix of populism, trades unionism, fascism and militarism. The rise of Juan Domingo Perón and the development of geometrical abstraction in Argentina are not unrelated at a structural level although of course, the two were mutually antagonistic.[3] There are important differences to note between the generation of 1944 and previous "modern" generations in Argentina. First of all, the young men and women who grouped together after the publication of *Arturo* were almost all Argentine-born, mostly of middle or working-class origins and, above all, had not travelled to Europe to "learn their trade" as artists. Many Argentine art historians insist that this generation has precedents in figures such as Emilio Pettoruti and Juan Del Prete, as these two artists frequently used abstraction as an element in their pictures, but in fact, there is a gulf separating the two generations. While it is true that Pettoruti's exhibition in 1924 provoked a riot in the gallery, nothing could have been further from his intentions, despite his stylistic flirtation with Futurism. Broadly speaking, the generation of the 1920s and 1930s used the visual devices of the European avant-garde which served, above all, to show their commitment to all that was new in Europe – although inevitably this always arrived late within the tight chronological scale of modern art. Understood thus, "modernism" in an Argentine context can be seen as little more than yet another way of sharing an élite culture with Europe.

The first and only issue of the "Arturo" journal 1944

1) The title is taken from a text printed on the inside back cover of *Arturo* magazine, which epitomises the desire of the geometrical artists to create a new Argentine culture, away from what many see as a particular Argentine tendency towards melancholia. The translations from Spanish are my own.

2) *Arturo, revista de artes abstractas* was edited by Arden Quin, Rhod Rothfuss, Gyula Kosice and Edgar Bayley with contributions by Joaquín Torres García, Vicente Huidobro, Murilo Mendes, Tomás Maldonado, Vieira da Silva, Augusto Torres, Lidy Maldonado (Pratí), Piet Mondrian and Vassily Kandinsky. The particular characteristics of the magazine – of which a facsimile is being published – are too complex to enter into here. In its symbolic value for a whole generation, *Arturo* is comparable to that of the magazine *Martín Fierro* in the 1920s.

3) An example of Peronist cultural policy is contained in a speech by the Minister of Education, Dr. Ivanissevich (reported in *La Nación* 22/9/49): "Morbid art, abstract art, has no place amongst us in this country flowering in its youth (…) Peronists have no time for Fauvists, less for Cubists, abstracts and Surrealists. A Peronist is a person of defined sex who admires beauty in all its senses." As Alberto Molenberg pointed out, abstract artists in Argentina were under attack from Peronism, Nazism and Stalinism (interview with the author, Buenos Aires, May 1993).

Invitation card to the exhibition
"Arte Concreto Invención"
by the photographer Grete Stern,
Buenos Aires 1945

*) In recent exhibitions of Latin American art, works
from the Arte Concreto/Madí period have not been
sufficiently controlled as regards their chronology. The
tendency for artists to ante-date their works has resulted
in considerable confusion as to the true development
of the movements as reflected in the contemporary
documentation. As yet, there are still parts of the
chronological sequence which are not fully resolved.

This does not apply to the works illustrated in this
catalogue (The editor).

4) The Galería Comte was part of an important modernist furniture store. An exhibition of Arte Concreto
with Arden Quin, Tomás and Lidy Maldonado, Kosice,
Manuel Espinosa and Rothfuss was announced but
accounts conflict as to the realisation of the exhibition.

5) A third issue of the magazine, *Sobre Arte Concreto*
by Tomás Maldonado was announced but never appeared.

6) The fact that these first exhibitions were in private
houses is significant. It proved very difficult for these
artists to enter commercial galleries, with a few exceptions like the Van Riel Gallery, which was used as a
regular venue. Parallel with this is an almost total lack
of interest on the part of local critics.

There is a new aggressive attitude to art and to history in the generation of *Arturo,*
along with a desire to participate fully in the dynamics of the avant-garde, despite
a marginal geographic position. An example of this is the questioning attitude
adopted towards the school of the constructivist Joaquín Torres García across the
River Plate in Montevideo [Uruguay]. Despite his impeccable credentials as a
participant in the most important European schools of geometrical abstraction
(Cercle et Carré, Abstraction-Création, etc.), his teachings, which were so
religiously followed by artists in Uruguay, were dealt with irreverently by the
Buenos Aires avant-garde. Through his age and experience Torres García would
have been the obvious mentor for the young artists; but, as I will illustrate, the
mutual animosity was considerable.

Unfortunately, the history of the rise of Arte Madí and the Asociación Arte Concreto-
Invención is all but lost in a sea of personal rivalries, ambitions and mystifications,
meaning that so far, most "histories" of the period are little more than loosely-veiled
defences of particular interests. This has also been accompanied in some recent
cases by the deliberate manufacture and exhibition of ante-dated works of art.* On
another, and more benevolent, level, the passionate urge to be on the side of History
is in itself revealing of the utopian transformative programme of which the artists
felt (and many indeed still feel) themselves to be a part.

The years 1944 to 1946 were extremely turbulent, not just in Argentine political
history but in the particular histories of the movements we are concerned with.
After the publication in Summer 1944 of *Arturo,* the original nucleus of artists
grouped and re-grouped many times, exhibiting once together in the Galería
Comte[4] before, by mid-1945, two main tendencies emerged.

One the one hand Carmelo Arden Quin, Gyula Kosice and Rhod Rothfuss grouped
together, while simultaneously Tomás Maldonado was bringing together students
from the National School of Fine Arts to form the Asociación Arte Concreto-
Invención. In 1945 two important issues of the magazine *Invención* appeared, the
first by Kosice, including photographs of his first articulated sculptures in wood
(such as *Röyi),* and the second by Edgar Bayley, the poet brother of Tomás
Maldonado.[5]

Two obscure but vital exhibitions took place in 1945 of the Kosice/Arden
Quin/ Rothfuss group: one in October in the house of Enrique Pichon-Rivière, one
of the leaders of the APA (Asociación Psicoanalítica Argentina), under the title *Art
Concret Invención* and another altogether more ambitious exhibition in the house
of the Bauhaus-trained photographer Grete Stern in December, now under the title
of *Movimiento de Arte Concreto-Invención.*[6] The Grete Stern exhibition established the multi-media exhibition as the norm for this group, which within six
months would call itself Madí.

Group-picture on the occasion of the
"Art Concret Invention" exhibition
by Dr. Pichon-Rivière in Buenos-Aires
1945. Second from left Arden Quin,
seated in the front Gyula Kosice, on the
far right Dr. Pichon-Rivière

A
R   I
T   N
C   V
O   E
N   N
C   T
R   I
E   O
T   N

8 - 10
1945

CHEZ PICHON - RIVIERE

SANTA FE 1379   BUENOS AIRES

Arden Quin, Carmelo
"Coplanal" 1945
Lacquer on panel, ca. 55 cm h.
(adjustable)
Private collection Basle
(cover illustration)

---

7) Recent research in Rivera/Sant'Ana do Livramento has shown that much of the generally-accepted story of Arden Quin's early life is inaccurate. Arden Quin's own version of events is contained in an interview published in *La República,* Montevideo (22.7.1992). At the time of writing, there is also no evidence of Kosice's origins or activity before the early 1940s. The ambiguity over personal details – and subsequent battle over them – is characteristic of many Madí artists and seems to reflect their peculiar sense of identity and origin.

8) This is further confirmed by an unsigned note – Aclaración – in the *2nd Bulletin of the Asociación Arte Concreto-Invención* (December 1946), page 2, which reads: "At this time, 1940, Mr. Arden Quin had no contact with abstract art of with painting (his first pictorial works are from 1945) and he was a surrealist poet; as regards Mr. Gyula Kosice, he had no contact with art in general (his first poetic experiments are those published in *Arturo* magazine, 1944, and his first objects, 1945)".

9) This split was cemented by a "Matinée Madiste" in April 1948 organised by Arden Quin and Blaszko. At this time there were two permanent Madí exhibitions: one at Kosice/Laañ's house and the other at Blaszko's.

10) Interview with the author, Paris, December 1992.

Arte Madí

Of the several movements to come out of *Arturo,* Madí has remained the most intriguing and difficult to classify to this day. While its rival movement, the Asociación Arte Concreto-Invención, adopted the language and practices of respectability, Madí was always more concerned with Dada-like mobilisations and declarations than with the isolated aesthetic qualities of the works produced.

This is not the place to enter into the interminable debates over the foundation of the Madí Movement or the origins of the name. The most violent debate centres over the "invention" of the Madí idea. Accounts vary as to the exact date of arrival of the Uruguayan Carmelo Arden Quin in Buenos Aires, the point his followers use as the start of Madí. While he has dated it to 1938, there is no record of his activity at this time. Also, the dating of "cut frame" works from the 1930s and early 1940s appears to have no solid documentary basis.[7] The weight of evidence at the time of writing lies against any pictorial production before 1944, about the time he entered into contact with Rhod Rothfuss.[8]

When Arden Quin arrived in Buenos Aires he was considerably older than the group of artists he associated with, and brought with him a knowledge of Dialectical Materialism and primitive art which informs his early writings and which greatly influenced many artists of his set. Arden Quin's early works have recently been reassessed after a long period of obscurity, and show a remarkable sense of form and colour in paintings which are somehow more suggestive and seductive than the harsher works of contemporaries like Rothfuss, Diyi Laañ and Kosice. Arden Quin's philosophy of art is heavily influenced by Torres García, in contrast to the rest of his generation (the other exception being Alfredo Hlito). However, his interest in Dialectical Materialism led to his taking several key concepts and systems from Torres García and deleloping them along Marxist lines. Arden Quin's work from the period shows less of a dogmatic commitment to the purist aesthetic, but in turn a greater freedom to experiment with the elements of art in a more playful way. Of the Madí artists, Arden Quin can be seen as the most influenced by European trends.

With the benefit of hindsight, one can see the inevitable initial attraction between Arden Quin, Rothfuss and Kosice, and also the eventual violent parting of ways. By 1947 and the publication of the first issue of Kosice's magazine *Arte Madí Universal,* Arden Quin and Martin Blaszko had split away from the main group,[9] and Arden Quin's commitment in any case was less constant as he confesses to always dreaming of settling in Paris,[10] which he did in 1948. On the other hand, in its foundation, it seems that Madí came from the meeting of these three strong personalities, and it was precisely this mixture with all its conflict and contradictions which gave Madí its unique qualities.

By June 1946, the name Madí was being used on broadsheets distributed freely in the streets of Buenos Aires spelling out their aims. Other broadsheets were printed on self-adhesive paper to stick on the Buenos Aires public transport system, an early example of Madí's remarkable flair for publicity.

The first exhibition of the group under this name (Arden Quin, Kosice and Rothfuss had exhibited in 1945 in the houses of Pichon-Rivière and Grete Stern), was in August 1946 at the French Institute of Higher Education. From the catalogue of this event, we see a list of fourteen "members of Madí".[11] In fact this is a common Madí tactic: using pseudonyms and names of people only tangentially associated with the movement to pad out the list of names.[12] The desire to name objects in an original manner can be traced above all to Gyula Kosice, who is something of a master at inventing names, from his important sculpture of 1944 which he called *Röyi* to the *Portable Madí Dictionary,* which consists of invented words with equally invented definitions.[13]

The first Madí exhibition was in fact more of a performance than an exhibition in the traditional sense. Over three days, one could attend dance performances, concerts, and poetry readings. On the first day, Carmelo Arden Quin read an "Introduction to the Manifesto" sparking off a fierce controversy over the authorship of the *Madí Manifiesto.* To this day there is no conclusive proof one way or the other, but it is clear that the text which has reached us today is the earliest published version, and that it bears a stronger link to the Kosice/Rothfuss group of artists on documentary, stylistic and ideological grounds.[14]

Rhod Rothfuss remains an enigma. An apparently contradictory character, with a common Uruguayan mixture of bohemia and scholarship along with the typical addiction to mate infusions, his role in the foundation of the Madí movement was central. It was Rothfuss who in *Arturo* (1944) published his article "The Frame: a problem in contemporary art',[15] which established the theoretical base for the Argentine avant-garde: the irregular frame which allows the edge of the picture plane to be determined by the edge of the pictorial composition. As he wrote: "A painting with a regular frame suggests an extension of the subject which only disappears when the frame is rigorously constructed according to the composition of the painting". Rothfuss, unlike Kosice and Arden Quin, was a trained artist and earned his living teaching. Unfortunately, little remains of Rothfuss's production — approximately ten paintings and one sculpture.[16] From the accompanying illustration to his article in *Arturo* magazine, we can see that his development of the cut frame came through semi-figurative Cubist paintings, of which only one remains.[17] However, by 1946 his style became clearer and more assertive, painting in blocks of colour isolated visually from each other with black bands. Rothfuss was not an especially political animal, and he generally steered clear of the more

11)   Arden Quin, Gyula Kosice, Rhod Rothfuss, Martin Blaszko, Valdo W. Longo, Diyi Laañ, Elisabeth Steiner, Ricardo Humbert, Alejandro Havas, Dieudonné Costes, Raymundo Rasas Pét, Sylwan-Joffe Lemme, Esteban Eitler, Paulina Ossona. It is also worth noting that on the back of the programme is printed: "Leaders of Madí: Arden Quin, Gyula Kosice, Rhod Rothfuss".

12)   Much controversy surrounds the use of pseudonyms. In an attempt to set the record straight: Arden Quin's real name is Carmelo Heriberto Alves (sheet 138v, book A-18, Registro Civil, Sant'Ana do Livramento -RS- Brazil), Gyula Kosice's civil name is Fernando Fallik (DNI, Policía Federal Argentina No. 2168961), and Rhod Rothfuss was born Carlos María Rothfuss (No. 500), Registro Civil, 18a Sección de Montevideo). As regards pseudonyms, Sylwan-Joffe Lemme and Dieudonnè Costes were adopted by Arden Quin; Raymundo Rasas Pet is Kosice, as can be seen by the articles signed with this name in all the issues of Kosice's journal *Arte Madí Universal* from 1947 to 1954 and also by tracing works published under this name to a series of photographs of Kosice's work taken by Grete Stern c. 1946. Most of the orther names can all be traced other than Alejandro Havas, who remains enigmatic, with a single photograph published in 1953. However, drawing published under this name bear no stylistic similarity to the work of either Kosice or Arden Quin.

13)   Diccionario Madi in *Arte Madí Universal,* No. 2, Buenos Aires, October 1948.

14)   To sketch out some of the main events surrounding the *Madí Manifiesto* (full text in Dawn Ades: *Art in Latin America,* 1989, Appendix 11.3): 3rd August 1946 – Arden Quin reads *Introducción al Manifiesto* at 1st Madí exhibition, no record remains of what he read. In 1947, a *Manifiesto de la escuela* is published in Spanish and French in the first issue of *Arte Madí Universal,* but is unsigned and undated. This is the text we know as the *Madí Manifiesto.* In 1947, the text appears in the same form in French as a broadsheet, now signed by Kosice and with the name Madinemsor, which Kosice invented in 1947 to differentiate his group. In 1948, the text appeared in English in the 2nd issue of *Arte Madí Universal* and is dated 1946-7. Arden Quin made no claims to the authorship of this text until the 1980s, when he printed his initial, slightly different version of the text, claiming Kosice had appropriated and changed it. The flaw of Arden Quin's argument is the failure to produce the original document from which he transcribed this text after over thirty years. In conclusion, the authorship can not be attributed exactly and the text can be dated to 1947. This is not to say it was not written or signed earlier, simply that at the time of writing, there is no documented proof. However, the text was the unchallenged manifesto of the Kosice/Rothfuss group for the time Madí existed, supporting Kosice's claim to authorship.

15)   Text in English in D. Ades, *Art in Latin America* (1989), appendix 11.2.

16)   Fortunately, his work was documented in the magazine *Arte Madí Universal.*

17)   Collection Gyula Kosice, Buenos Aires.

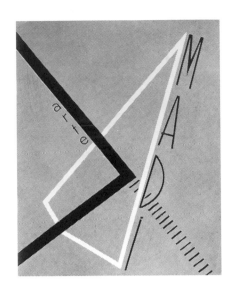

Issue No 6, 1952 of "Arte MADI Universal" a journal edited by Gyula Kosice

bombastic activities of the Madí group. In the testimony of his friend, the sculptor Horacio Faedo: "I remember popping in at any time and sharing his mate amargo (always freshly prepared) and always finding him humble and straightforward, as though what he was doing were not even worthwhile, with his pencil, paintbrush, set square, compass and Golden Section compass".[18]

Another artist with a similar dedication to his calling is the sculptor and painter Martin Blaszko. Blaszko's early paintings are greatly influenced by Carmelo Arden Quin, although while Arden Quin changed styles and formats continually, Blaszko continued to refine his blocks of colour within a cut frame through the 1940s. Never claiming a leading role in the Madí movement, Blaszko's attitude has been of more serious dedication to his art. In the 1950s he turned his attention to sculpture, and in particular to the urban environment.

While Gyula Kosice was the organisational motor behind the Buenos Aires Madí movement, editor of the fascinating magazine *Arte Madí Universal* (eight issues: 1947–54) and creator of most of Madí's peculiar language and style, nonetheless he deserves to be considered apart from the main group. It is my view that, of all the artists of the generation of 1944, Kosice represents the most disconcerting and interesting tendency of his group: the freedom to move between historical styles and tendencies without becoming slave to any. Kosice's production is marked by an interstellar utopianism which remains constant from his declaration in *Arturo* that "El hombre no ha de terminar en la tierra" (Mankind will not be exhausted on Planet Earth), through his project for the Hydrospatial City to his recent sculptures. In Kosice there is an almost biological reaction against traditional art, combined with a refusal to distinguish between art and life.[19]

While poetry was an important element for the Argentine avant-garde of the 1940s, with Edgar Bayley developing "Inventionist" poetry, as a rule this poetry was more an amalgamation of Surrealism, Dadaism and *creacionismo* than anything radically new. In contrast, in Kosice's case, it is vital to consider his poetry when analysing the originality of his proposals. In *Densidad del paisaje abandonado* (Density of the abandoned landscape), published in *Arturo,* he finishes the poem:

> *Promedio retención*
> *exposición durable*
> *Latitud 0'08791*

18) H. Faedo, "Un momento con Rothfuss", dictated to the author, Colonia del Sacramento, Uruguay, June 1993.

19) Kosice dates this desire for integration to his early contact with the ideas of Leonardo da Vinci and their emotional impact during his adolescence. Interview with the author, Buenos Aires, April 1993.

This degree of freedom from traditional word/meaning relationships, while avoiding Surrealist connotations, is something quite new in Argentina. Throughout the 1940s, Kosice fought a Quixotic battle against Surrealism, claiming always that art had to be a product of conscious thought and visionary scientific imagination.

Kosice's early works are constructions from materials he found in the leather workshop he ran with his brothers. These early, fragile works were recorded photographically by Grete Stern, and show the different interests of the young Kosice with regard to his contemporaries.

In his enthusiasm to reject contemporary European artistic conventions, allied to his naturally provocative personality, Kosice engaged in a propaganda war against the other representatives of the avant-garde, basing himself on Rothfuss's doctrine of the irregular frame. In particular, he was critical of the Zurich school of concrete art (and by extension, the Asociación Arte Concreto-Invención), and has always religiously insisted on the "difference" of Madí. For example, he has written: "Our aim was not to establish a 'geometrical order' like Neoplasticism, nor to search for an objective expression of reality which would 'signify' rationality, rigour, purity and uncontamination in opposition to the idea of art as 'expression' of emotions, the unconscious, social reality, primitivism, etc. (…) neither did we want a mere exaltation of visual 'values', which leads to a pedantic and empty form of interior decoration, but rather a deep reflection and desire for action on the aesthetic act, and also on Man's existential condition on Planet Earth".[20]

Kosice's search for integration of the arts and a new humanism of the twentieth century led to his proposal for the Hydrospatial City in the 1970s. The idea is to create a habitat suspended in space (the first to be above the River Plate) where Mankind will be free to experience life in such a radically transformed habitat that there will no longer be any need to have separate art works as such. Supposedly, the experience of art will be dissolved into the way of life. The source of these ideas can be directly traced to the 1940s and his first declarations in *Arturo:* "If distances are abolished, Art will be just tension, and image will be pure aesthetic vibration".[21] From his very first works, Kosice was always more interested in the transformative, mobile aspects of art and in pushing back the frontiers of our notions of what constitutes a "sculpture". His revolutionary sculpture *Röyi* shows this principle in its refusal to conform to a single compositional arrangement. By the late 1940s, Kosice began to experiment with water as the ultimate transformative element and throughout the 1950s and '60s worked almost exclusively with what he calls "hydrosculpture", reinforcing his cosmic utopian theories with manifestos, poems and articles.

Kosice's use of materials has been equally revolutionary. The use of glass led to his adopting plexiglass or acrylic, often along with aluminium, wood, cork, bone, and many other unexpected materials. From his experiments with glass and his interest in science, motion and electricity, he had the idea of creating sculptures purely from light itself, and thus made reliefs in neon, predating experiments elsewhere in the world.

Kosice, Gyula
"Röyi", 1944, adjustable sculpture,
wood, 120 x 80 x 25 cm
Private collection Buenos Aires

20) G. Kosice, "Continuo de Arte Madí A treinta y seis años de una fundación esencial", in Kosice, *Arte Madí,* Buenos Aires, 1982, p. 12–13.

21) G. Kosice, "Afirmaciones de Arturo", *Arturo* magazine, Buenos Aires, 1944.

"Arte Concreto-Invención"
No 1, August 1946

22) In the *Bulletin* of the group published in December 1946, the date of formation of the Asociación is confirmed as November 1945. It is also worth noticing that Mele, Vardánega and Villalba were exhibiting in their studio on the Avenue Juan B. Justo in 1945.

23) The political commitment and style of the Asociación can be seen in their statutes of November 1946. For example: "Inventionism claims solidarity with all the peoples of the world and their great ally: the Soviet Union". However, it remains difficult to establish the exact relationship of the Asociación with the Communist Party. I am very grateful to Agnès de Maistre for providing the statutes and several other previously lost documents of the Asociación.

24) The text in English is available in Dawn Ades's *Art in Latin America* London, 1989, Appendix 11.4.

25) T. Maldonado, "Torres García contra el arte moderno", *Boletín de la Asociación Arte Concreto-Invención*, No. 2, Buenos Aires, December 1946, p. 1.

The Asociación Arte Concreto-Invención

While Kosice identified himself totally and exclusively with Madí and by extension with the whole avant-garde, Madí is only part of the story. Around 1945, concurrently with the exhibitions organised by the Madí artists, another group was forming around Tomás Maldonado and the National School of Fine Arts. The initial group consisted of Maldonado, Alfredo Hlito, Claudio Girola, Enio Iommi, Lidy Pratí, Manuel Espinosa, Raúl Lozza, Alberto Molenberg and others, and shortly afterwards Juan Mele, Virgilio Villalba and Gregorio Vardánega. The exact date of formation of the Asociación Arte Concreto-Invención, as the group called itself, is unknown, but many observers date it to November 1945.[22] From the outset there was considerable rivalry between the two groups, based largely on a clash of personality, aims and, above all, artistic practice. The members of the Asociación were always more visual artists in a traditional sense, not expanding into other activities and insisting on the pictorial qualities of the works themselves. Although their first works adopted the irregular frame practice, the true precursor oth the "shaped canvas", proposed by Rothfuss in *Arturo* (1944) and central to the Madí movement, their aesthetic gradually led them back to the rectangular frame. The Asociación, rather than engaging in the permanent squabbles and polemics of Madí, worked as a collective movement, politically committed to Communism and discussing aesthetic issues in committees.[23]

In the 1940s, the Asociación Arte Concreto-Invención represented another attempt to bring Argentina up to date, to participate in a perceived modernist, utopian "project", just as rationalist architects such as Alberto Prebisch and composers like Juan Carlos Paz had done in other fields. It is in this light that we should also approach their declared collective allegiance to the Communist party and to the Soviet Union, as the political expression of the perceived inevitable force of change and the desire to be on the side of historical forces.

Because of this practical commitment to rationalism, the aesthetic history of the Asociación has a clearer structure; from the cut frame, the forms gradually became more independent of one another, resulting ultimately in the physical separation in space of the forms connected by plastic rods (the first work of this type was Molenberg's *Función Blanca).* After this, the debate centred around the problem of controlling the exact relationships of the painted elements when the wall was allowed to interfere visually with the composition. As a result of this debate, around 1948, the artists moved towards different solutions concerning the resolution of the edge of the picture plane. For artists such as Maldonado and Hlito (partly as a result of Maldonado's contact in 1948 with Max Bill and Vantongerloo in Europe), the solution was to return to painted forms on a rectangular canvas which, in its least original form, produced little more than pastiches of the Zurich

School; while for others such as Lidy Pratí it released greater possibilities. Both Juan Mele and Vardánega moved towards a greater exploration of space and relief; Mele by separating forms physically above a white canvas and Vardánega by working in spherical forms, until eventually in the 1950s he stepped into the field of Kinetic Art. For some artists, such as Alfredo Hlito, the Concrete Art period provided a necessary training (or "military service" in the words of Jorge Romero Brest) before he found his true artistic freedom in a more painterly abstraction from the mid-1950s. The first exhibition of the Asociación Arte Concreto-Invención took place in the Peuser Gallery in March 1946. The manifesto of the group, called the *Inventionist Manifiesto*,[24] was published with the programme and signed by the Asociación's sixteen members, although Maldonado and Bayley's authorship is generally recognised. The manifesto is an attack on the principle of illusionism in traditional art and declares the aim to "surround man with real things and not ghosts (…) to accustom Man to relate directly to objects and not to the fiction surrounding objects (…) For a precise aesthetic, an exact technique. Aesthetic function against "good taste". White function. Neither Searching nor Finding: Invention".

In August of the same year, the Asociación published its first journal, *Arte Con creto-Invención,* with theoretical texts by Maldonado, Bayley, Contreras and Hlito and illustrated with the first irregular frame paintings of the group.

The second issue of the magazine appeared in December 1946, with no illustrations but reaffirming Maldonado, Hlito, Bayley and Lozza as the theorists of the movement. The cover page of the bulletin is a long attack on Torres García by Tomás Maldonado entitled "Torres García contra el Arte Moderno". In this article, Maldonado writes: "The real problem is that Torres García, stuck in the narrowness of his colonialist spirit, in the dusty archaisim of 'American curiosities' and indigenist 'pastiches', is incapable of appreciating the deep and emotive sense which lies in a white washable and lacquered surface".[25] This attack was, in its turn, a response to hostile articles published against the new Argentine avantgarde in *Removedor,* the organ of the *Taller Torres García* in Montevideo.[26] Contrary to what is generally stated, there was no love lost between the Argentine artists of 1944 and the school of Joaquín Torres García. Many Argentine artists who placed Mondrian, Van Doesburg and Malevich as their idols were disappointed at Torres's abandoning of the purist aesthetic in favour of his own particular brand of Americanism, mixing figurative and nonfigurative elements loosely based on a reinterpretation of primitive cultures. Both Maldonado, in the article quoted, and Gyula Kosice particularly criticised him for his insistence on the use of the Golden Section,[27] a concept to which Maldonado later returned but which Kosice rejected forever as another hangover from traditional concepts of art.

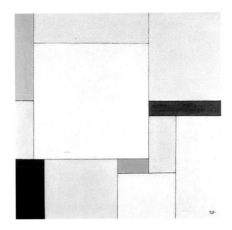

Vantongerloo, Georges
"Composition dans le carré", 1930
Oil on canvas, 50 x 50 cm
Private collection Switzerland

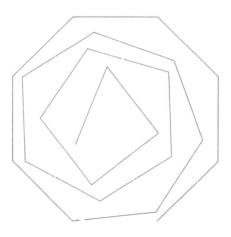

Bill, Max
"15 variations on a theme", 1935–1938

26) See: S. Cabrera, "Originalidad e Invención", *Removedor,* No. 14, Montevideo, 1946, for a direct attack on the Argentine groups.

27) Kosice claims that on a visit to Torres García in 1946, he took the model of his sculpture *Röyi* which Torres rejected for not having been composed with the Golden Section (interview with the author, Buenos Aires, April 1993). However, of the Madí artists, Blaszko, Rothfuss and Arden Quin used the Golden Section frequently as a compositional support.

"Perceptismo" periodical edited by
Raúl Lozza, No 1, October 1950

28) Aracy Amaral in *Latin American Artists of the Twentieth Century* (New York, 1993, p. 88) repeats the misattribution made in Nelly Perazzo's *El Arte Concreto en La Argentina* (Buenos Aires, 1983, p. 93) by including Alberto Molenberg as a member of the Perseptismo group. Interviews with Raúl Lozza and Alberto Molenberg, Buenos Aires, May 1993.

29) Interview with the author, Buenos Aires, May 1993. The title was probably suggested by the critic Abraham Haber, who was a member of the group and as well as publishing the book *Raúl Lozza y el Perceptismo* in 1948, contributed regularly to the magazine *Perceptismo* which appeared from 1950 to 1953.

30) R. Lozza, *Manifiesto Perceptista*, first published in October 1949, Van Riel Gallery.

31) *Cualimetría* is a neologism from *cualidad* (characteristic) and *geometría*. Lozza believes that traditional geometry is insufficient because it does not take into account the visual quality (illusionism) of the forms (Interview with the author, Buenos Aires, May 1993).

Perceptismo

As a result of the debates of the Asociación Arte Concreto-Invención, Raúl Lozza found his own solution,[28] a movement he called Perceptismo (by his own confession an arbitrary title)[29] which he launched in 1948 after separating from the Asociación in 1947. Lozza's theory takes the notions of objectivity and bi-dimensionality to their logical conclusions without reverting to European art practices. Perceptismo developed into a system where the objective elements of art – colour and form – are measured and balanced in order to cancel any effects of illusionism (recession).

While the other artists of the Asociación abandoned the "cut frame" as they realised it was impossible to control strictly the colour-form relationships of their paintings (the colour of the wall being allowed to interfere in the composition for example), Lozza found another solution: to make the support an essential, albeit provisional, part of the work of art.

Lozza's central concern is with integrating art with its particular relationships into architecture and the visual environment. Rothfuss's attack on the notion of the frame as a "window" (which gave birth to the cut frame) finds one of its most pure expressions in Lozza's calculated negation of all illusionism in art. By cancelling, through his own mathematical system, the visual effects of recession, a "portable wall" or support would be constructed to provide the correct colour base for each particular composition. To avoid the rectangular frame re-establishing the compositional limits of illusionism, Lozza's solution lies in the centrifugal nature of his compositions (estructura abierta), where the edge of the support is as large or small as one wishes, and would ideally be an architectural wall.

In his *Manifiesto Perceptista* of 1949, Lozza wrote: "It [Perseptismo] creates a new realist conception of functional structure; by transcending the old contradiction between form and content, it is basing itself on the dialectical method which is present in the very workings of matter".[30]

It is especially interesting to compare how Rothfuss's theory produced on the one hand Lozza's exaltation of the architecturally pure environment and, on the other, Kosice's project for the Hydrospatial City in which the traditional architectural system (including his greatest enemy: rationalist architecture) is totally eroded and negated in favour of a radically new utopian modus vivendi.

On the Non-Spiritual in Art

Raúl Lozza's Perceptismo represents the extreme example of a materialist philosophy of art, with its own mathematical system, *cualimetría,*[31] developed purely to cancel all unnecessary and suggestive elements in his compositions.

The *Inventionist Manifiesto* of 1946 declared that "the human spirit leaves its prehistoric condition" and that "A scientific aesthetic will replace the age-old speculative and idealist aesthetic". To many constructivist artists in Argentina, their mission was to herald a new age radically different from the "sentimental" and "melancholic" culture in which they lived. Indeed, this was an aim intrinsic to the very birth of geometrical abstraction in Europe. However, in its River Plate variant, one can detect the distinct absence of either Kandinsky's "inner necessity", Mondrian's theosophical "new spirit" or Malevich's "Supremacy of pure feeling in creative art". Instead, the inspiration seems to be the harshest, least compromising branch of this tradition: Concrete Art (founded by Theo van Doesburg in 1930), the Manifesto of which states: "A pictorial element has no other meaning than what it represents, consequently, the painting possesses no other meaning than what it is by itself.[32]

The rejection of the spirituality of abstraction is widespread in Argentina amongst geometrical artists to this day. Perhaps this is a result of the importation process itself. A significant anecdote concerns Alfredo Hlito's first contact with a real painting by Mondrian in Europe, where the realisation of how much painterly quality had been lost in reproduction provoked an artistic crisis resulting in his abandonment of geometry.[33] The occasional arrival of illustrations in books and magazines must have presented a rather disjointed vision of the process in Europe over the past forty years, and left the artists to "fill in the gaps" much more than many European artists would have had to do.

To say that the geometrical avant-garde in Argentina is the simple "importation" of artistic ideas of of another aesthetic, "bringing it up to date", would assume a more complete and regular arrival of information than there was and also ignores the reinterpretation and reconstruction of ideas which took place. Even in those cases where emulation was the declared aim, the final result could not possibly have the same set of meanings and associations as the original models. Despite the adoption of an apparently universal and rational language, one cannot but notice the difference in context and interpretation which took place in Argentina.

The Argentine avant-garde was hugely important as a precedent for the wave of Constructivism which subsequently spread across Latin America. Many of the characteristics noted appear again and again in different countries, especially what I have indicated as a peculiar concern with the visual image *per se*.[34] By 1950, the Argentine avant-garde was facing increasing international isolation (the rise of informalism in Europe) and local political opposition. The result was a series of more neutral associations (e.g. Arte Nuevo and Artistas modernos de la Argentina) which aimed to concentrate artists in a common de-politicised and less radical purpose.

By the early 1950s, the focus of interest shifts away from Argentina to Uruguay. In

32) "Art Concret. The basis of concrete painting", *Art Concret* No. 1, April 1930. Signed by Carlsrund, Doesburg, Hélion, Tutundjian, Wantz. In Joost Baljeu, *Theo van Doesburg*, London, 1974, p. 180–181. It is worth noting that this movement lasted little more than a year.

33) I am grateful to Martha Nanni for her information on Alfredo Hlito.

34) Certainly, there are exceptions. We have seen how Madí's aims were more varied yet we see similar concerns re-appear in a different form in Brazilian neoconcretism from the late 1950s (Helio Oiticica, Lygia Clark, etc.) and in the utopian yet local aims of *tropicalia*. There are many parallels to explore here.

35) In Uruguay, interest is still concentrated on the faithful disciples of Torres García, overshadowing such interesting constructivists as Costigliolo and Freire. The almost total lack of information on the Uruguayan Madí artists (Rothfuss, Uricchio) owes much to this neglect. I am very grateful to María Freire for her agenerosity in providing documentary material and information on this period.

Montevideo in 1952, a new group was formed by José Pedro Costigliolo and María Freire called Arte No-Figurativo. This group absorbed several of the Uruguayan Madí artists (Rothfuss, Llorens, Urrichio), but its characteristics were vastly different. Sadly, little research has been done on this fascinating group and its members.[35] From Uruguay we can trace the "wave" to Brazil, where the artists received great support from sponsors like the critic Mario Pedrosa, a type of support absent in Argentina until the days of the Di Tella Institute. By the 1960s, Kinetic Art had become the unofficial emblem of oil-rich Venezuela.

The obscurity surrounding the Generation of 1944 is no accident. There are many aspects which appear profoundly to disturb art historians, critics, and members of the public. It is significant that, at the time of writing, no works of the Madí group are on permanent show in Argentina, and to my knowledge, only one collector has the works on his walls in full view. In Argentina, the historical avant-garde has not yet been institutionalised as it has been in Europe and North America. As such, it retains its original power to shock and confuse in its own context.

Gabriel Pérez-Barreiro.

This essay was first published in the catalogue "Argentina 1920–1994", Museum of Modern Art, Oxford 1994

Carmelo Arden Quin

Juan Bay

Martín Blaszko

Claudio Girola

Alfredo Hlito

Enio Iommi

Gyula Kosice

Raúl Lozza

Tomás Maldonado

Juan Mele

Lidy Prati

Volf Roitman

Rhod Rothfuss

Gregorio Vardanega

Virgilio Villalba

All works not otherwise marked are the property of Galerie von Bartha, Basle, Switzerland

Foto Andrée Girard

Catalogue of the exhibition
"Arte Nuevo" Buenos Aires 1955

CARMELO ARDEN QUIN

(b. 1913, Rivera, Uruguay)

In 1932 began to study painting and history of art under Catalan writer and painter Emilio Sans. Met Joaquín Torres-García, 1935; in 1938 to Buenos Aires to study philosophy and law. Collaborated with group of vanguard writers and painters on review *Sinesia,* and in 1942 with poets Gedo Iommi and Edgard Bayley co-founded bimonthly *El Universitario.* Following year, with Bayley, Gyula Kosice, Tomás Maldonado and Lidy Pratí, formed group "Arturo" and later foundermember of "Arte Concreto-Invención", and Madí movement which succeeded it; influential in creation of Madí ideas, 1946, with Kosice and Madí group. In Paris, exhibited Salon des Réalités Nouvelles, 1949–1956. In Buenos Aires 1956, co-founded Association of New Art. Represented in the "Arte Concreto-Invención – Arte Madí" exhibition in Zurich 1991 and further in the exhibitions of Latin American Art: "Artistas Latino-americanos del siglo XX" starting in Sevilla 1992, then in Centre Georges Pompidou, Paris 1992–1993, in Museum Ludwig, Cologne 1993 and in the Museum of Modern Art, New York 1993. Also represented in the exhibition "Argentina 1920–1994" in Museum of Modern Art, Oxford 1994. Lives and works near Paris.

Arden Quin, Carmelo
"Instrument plastique" 1945
Wood and cord, 45,5 x 61 cm
Musée de Grenoble, France

Arden Quin, Carmelo
"Ivry" 1946
Wood, 24 x 47 cm
Private collection

Arden Quin, Carmelo
"Plan vert" 1945
Gouache on card, 41 x 29 cm

Arden Quin, Carmelo
"MadIA" 1945
Oil on card, 26 x 67 cm

Arden Quin, Carmelo
"Cheval" 1946
Oil on card, 50 x 31,5 cm

Arden Quin, Carmelo
"Mécanique" 1947
Lacquer on card, 55 x 41 cm
Collection
R. A. Grüneisen, Buenos Aires

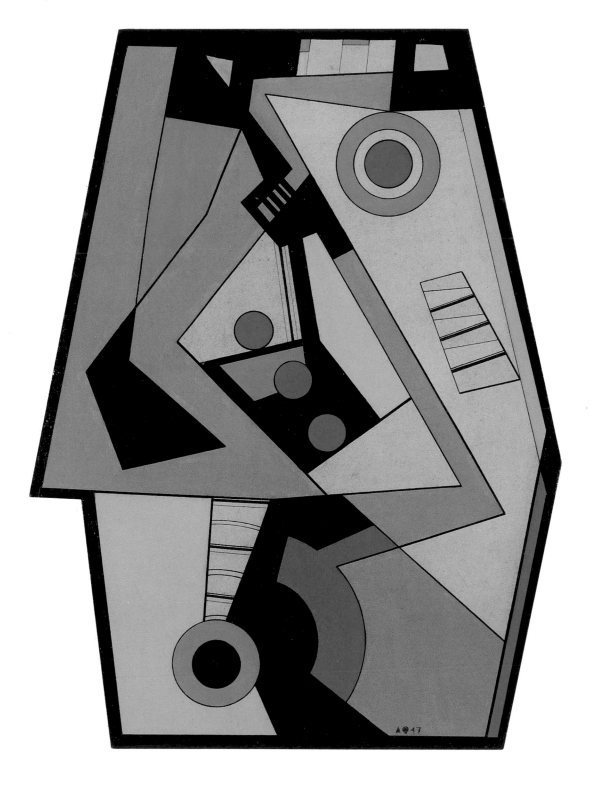

Arden Quin, Carmelo
"Structures 3" 1947
Lacquer on card, 47 x 66 cm
Private collection Zürich

Arden Quin, Carmelo
"Lignes et points" 1950
Painted panel, 90 x 38 x 2,5 cm
Private collection Germany

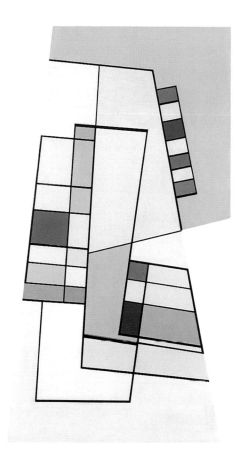

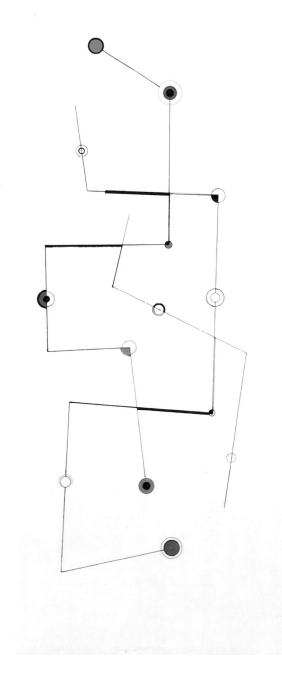

Arden Quin, Carmelo
"Trio 2" 1951
Lacquer on panel, 51 x 27 x 2,5 cm

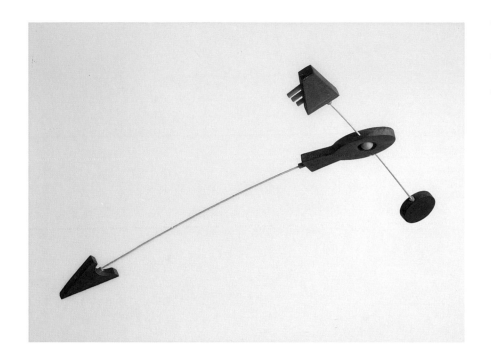

Arden Quin, Carmelo
Mobile 1948
Wood and metal, 90 x 75 cm

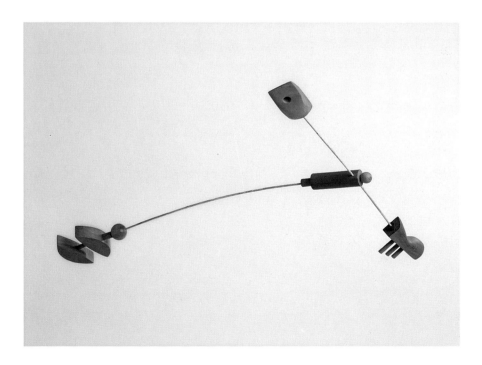

Arden Quin, Carmelo
Mobile 1948
Wood and metal, 80 x 82 cm

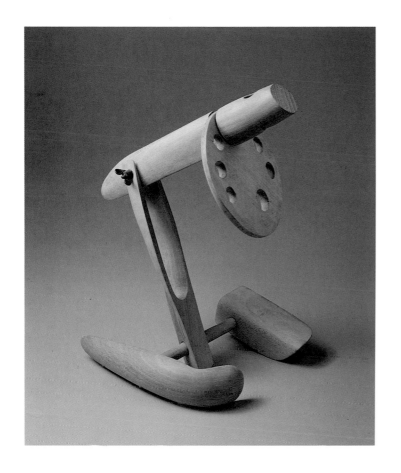

Arden Quin, Carmelo
Adjustable sculpture 1952
Wood, 45 cm high
Private collection Germany

Arden Quin, Carmelo
Adjustable sculpture 1952
Wood, 35 cm high
Private collection Germany

JUAN BAY

(b. 1892, Trenque Lauquén, Argentina – d. 1978)

Born in a province of Buenos Aires, moved to Milan, Italy, 1908. Studied painting and drawing until 1914; exhibited in the *Free Exhibition of Art* organized by the Futurists, Milan, 1911. In Argentina, 1925–1929. Again in Milan, was an active member of "Grupo del Milione"; wrote art criticism for European and Argentine periodicals. Invited to exhibit with the Futurists in the 1942 Venice Biennale and at the 1943 Cuadrienal de Roma. Returned to Argentina, 1949, and joined "Movimiento Madí", with whose artists he exhibited at Buenos Aires galleries and in the *Exposición en Resistencia,* and in Paris at the Denis René Gallery (1954–1958). Included in the exhibition *50 años de Pintura Argentina* (1951), Librería Viscontea, Buenos Aires, 1957, and the First Exhibition of Modern Art at the Museum of Modern Art, Buenos Aires (1960); retrospective. Represented in the "Arte Concreto-Invención – Arte Madí" exhibition in Zurich 1991 and in the exhibitions of Latin American Art: "Artistas Latino-americanos del siglo XX" starting in Sevilla 1992, then in Centre Georges Pompidou, Paris 1992–1993, in Museum Ludwig, Cologne 1993 and in the Museum of Modern Art, New York 1993. Also represented in the exhibition "Argentina 1920–1994" in Museum of Modern Art, Oxford 1994.

Bay, Juan
no title ca. 1950
Oil on panel, 43,5 cm
Private collection New York

Bay, Juan
"Composition MADI" ca. 1950
Painted panel, 81 x 57 cm

MARTIN BLASZKO

(b. 1920, Berlin)

In 1933, he left Germany, passing through several countries, until arriving in Argentina in 1939. In Argentina, his meeting, in 1945, with Carmelo Arden Quin, was formative. In that same year, Blaszko took up the practice of painting within an irregular frame. In 1946, he exhibited his paintings at the first Madí exhibition. In 1947, he started working in sculpture, where he found his true vocation. By the 1950s, Blaszko had moved away from the strict rectilinear geometry of his Madí works and started to experiment with a more dynamic, organic use of forms. In 1952, he won a prize for his project for the Monument to the Unknown Prisoner competition held at the Institute for Contemporary Arts, London, and the Tate Gallery. In 1968, he published "Sculpture and the Principle of Bipolarity" in Leonardo Magazine, Oxford, in which he explains his compositional theory. Blaszko's life-long concern has been with monumental sculpture and the urban environment. Represented in the "Arte Concreto-Invención – Arte Madí" exhibition in Zurich 1991 and the exhibitions of Latin American Art: "Artistas Latino-americanos del siglo XX" starting in Sevilla 1992, then in Centre Georges Pompidou, Paris 1992–1993, in Museum Ludwig, Cologne 1993 and in the Museum of Modern Art, New York 1993. He works as a sculptor in Buenos Aires.

Blaszko, Martin
"Ritmos verticales" 1947
Oil on panel, 93 x 44 cm

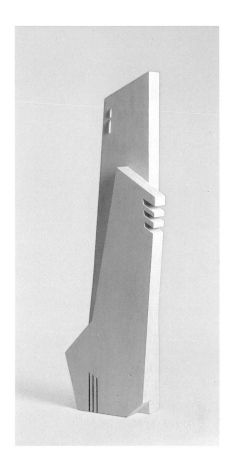

Blaszko, Martin
"Columna MADI" 1947
Painted wood, 75 cm high
Collection E. F. Costantini, Buenos Aires

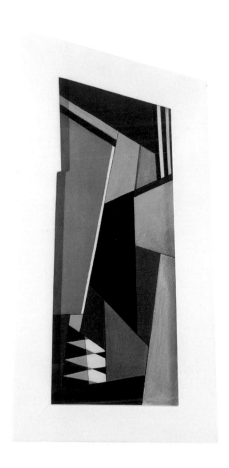

Blaszko, Martin
"Dinamica MADI" 1948
Oil on canvas, 49,5 x 19,5 cm
Private collection Zurich

Blaszko, Martin
"Armonía en verde" 1951
Oil on canvas, 58 x 37,5 cm
Private collection Luzern

Blaszko, Martin
"El gran ritmo" 1949
Oil on canvas, 93 x 43 cm
Collection
E. F. Costantini, Buenos Aires

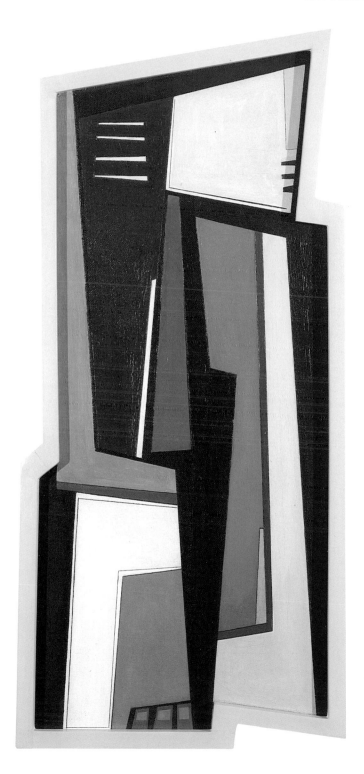

CLAUDIO GIROLA

(b. 1923, Rosario, Argentina – d. 1994, Santiago de Chile)

Parents Italian, father a sculptor and carver. Studied Manuel Belgrano School of Fine Arts, Buenos Aires; left 1943. Founding member with Iommi, Hlito and Maldonado of "Arte Concreto-Invencíon", 1945; in group show, Galería Peuser, 1946. To Europe, 1949; in Paris, met Vantongerloo; solo exhibition, Librería Salto, Milan, and showed with Milanese "Gruppo MAC". In Buenos Aires, 1952, exhibited with "Artistas Modernos de Argentina" at Galería Viau, and in 1953 at Galería Krayd. Member, Institute of Art, University of Valparaiso, Chile, 1952; exhibited Catholic University of Valparaiso. Moved to Valparaiso, 1957; retrospective, National Museum of Fine Arts, Santiago, Chile, 1961. Included in 1960 exhibition, 50 Años de Arte Argentino, National Museum of Fine Arts, Buenos Aires; received that Museum's Braque Prize, 1963. Represented in Venice Biennale, 1962, and Amsterdam Biennale, 1970; solo exhibitions, Buenos Aires, at Galería Rubbers, 1970, 1972, 1977, Galería Carmen Waugh, 1974 and Galería del Retiro 1983–1985. Collaborated on journal, *Revue de Poésie* (Paris).

Girola, Claudio
"Triangulos espaciales" 1948
Aluminium, 54 cm high

ALFREDO HLITO

(b. 1923, Buenos Aires – d. 1993)

Studied at the Escuela Nacional de Bellas Artes from 1938 to 1942. He was one of the leading painters and theorists of the Asociación Arte Concreto-Invención. He was a founder member of the Asociación Arte Concreto-Invención and signed the *Inventionist Manifiesto* of 1946. In 1951 he was involved in the foundation, with Maldonado, of *Nueva Visión* magazine, to which he frequently contributed. From 1955, he was constantly experimenting with different visual languages in works which made him one of Argentina's most respected modern painters. His later works are characterised by their painterliness. In 1964 he moved to Mexico, where he lived until 1973. His career was fully surveyed in a retrospective at the Museo Nacional de Bellas Artes in 1987. Represented in the "Arte Concreto-Invención – Arte Madí" exhibition in Zurich 1991 and further in the extensive series of exhibitions of Latin American Art: "Artistas Latino-americanos del siglo XX" starting in Sevilla 1992, then in Centre Georges Pompidou, Paris 1992–1993, in Museum Ludwig, Cologne 1993 and in the Museum of Modern Art, New York 1993. Also represented in the exhibition "Argentina 1920–1994" in Museum of Modern Art, Oxford 1994.

Hlito, Alfredo
"Ritmos cromaticos" 1947
Oil on canvas, 70 x 70 cm
Private collection Geneva

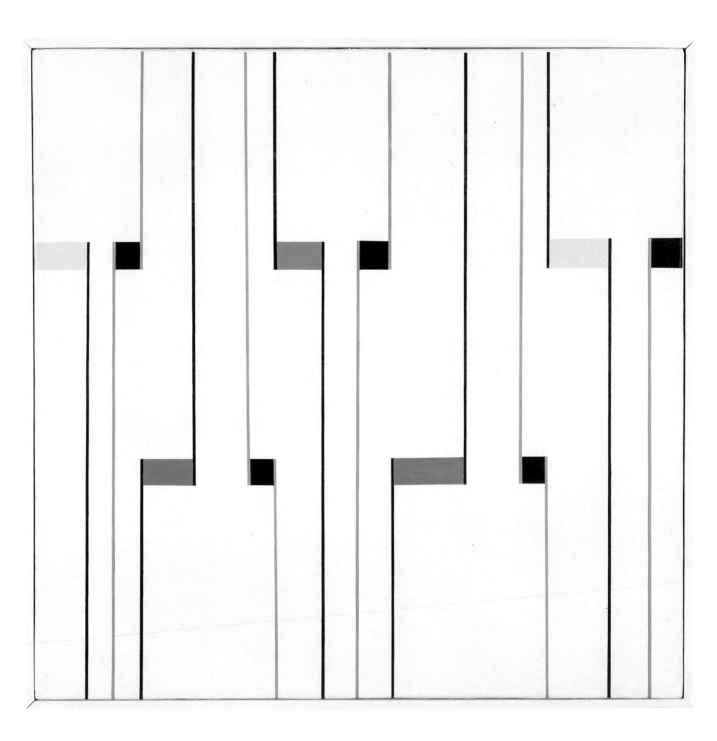

Hlito, Alfredo
"Series cromaticas" 1948
Oil on canvas, 100 x 100 cm
Private collection Zurich

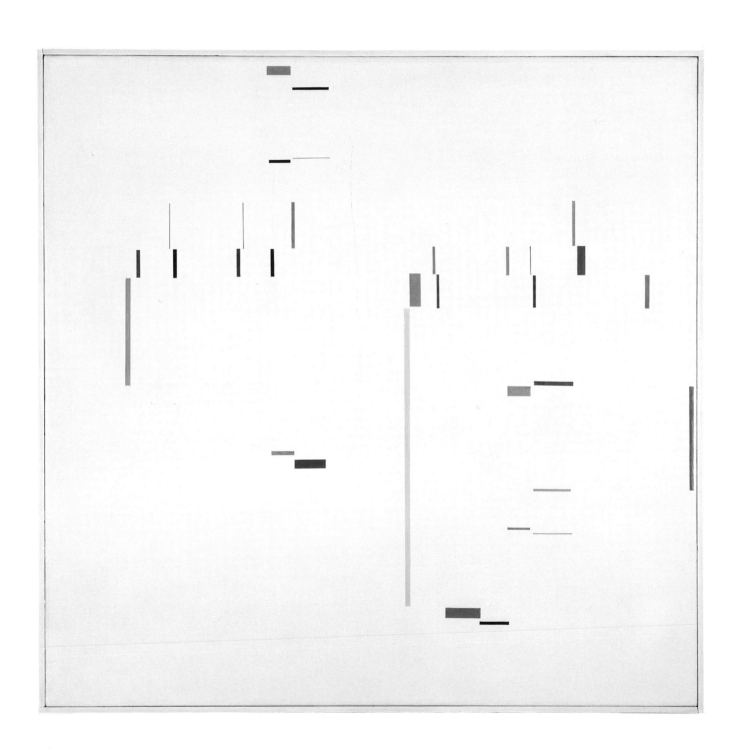

Hlito, Alfredo
"Ritmos cromaticos III" or
"Estructura y bandas" 1949
Oil on canvas, 100 x 100 cm
Barry Friedman Ltd. New York

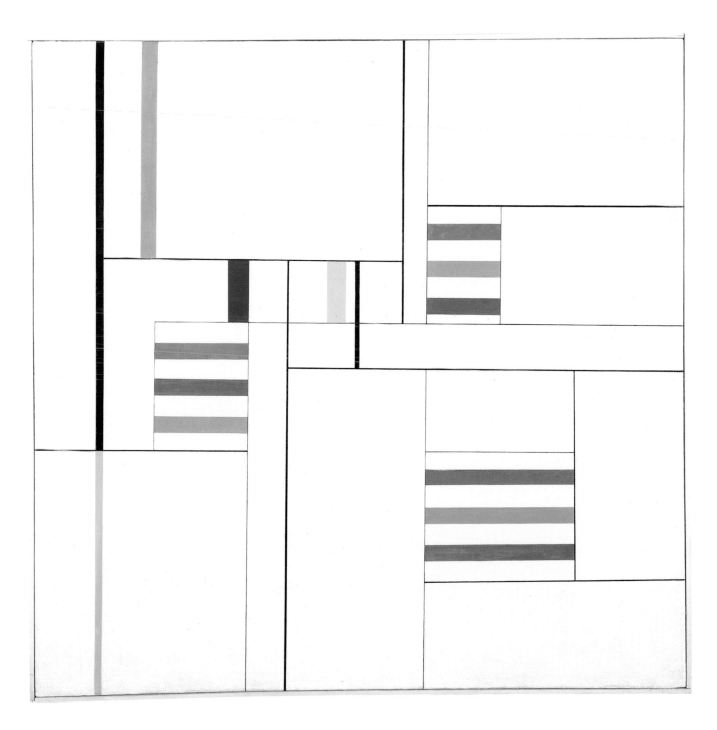

Hlito, Alfredo
"Elementos cromaticos" 1947
Oil on canvas, 65 x 55 cm
Private collection Switzerland

Hlito, Alfredo
"Curvas y series rectas" 1948
Oil on canvas, 70 x 70 cm
Barry Friedman Ltd. New York

Hlito, Alfredo
"Estructura sobre fondo amarillo" 1950
Oil on canvas, 55 x 45 cm
Private collection Switzerland

Hlito, Alfredo
"Development of a theme" 1952
Oil on canvas, 60 x 70 cm

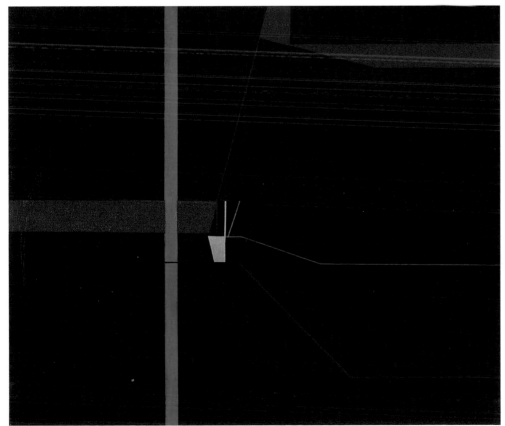

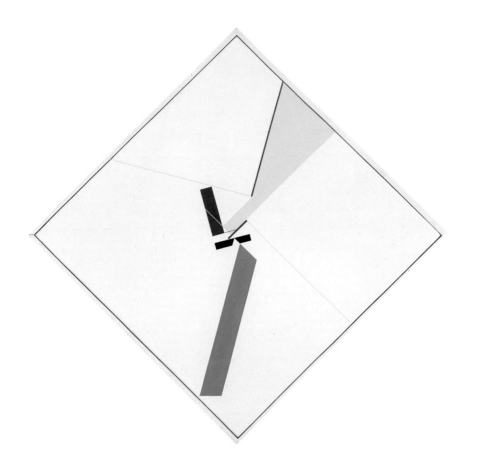

Hlito, Alfredo
"Reabsorción del rombo" 1953
Oil on canvas, 50 x 50 cm
Private collection Switzerland

Works by Alfredo Hlito in the exhibition
of modern Argentine art in Museo de
Arte Moderna in Rio de Janeiro, 1954

Hlito, Alfredo
Gouache 1952
44 x 30 cm
Private collection Germany

Hlito, Alfredo
Gouache 1953
35 x 25,5 cm
Private collection Germany

Hlito, Alfredo
"Volutas" 1956/57
Oil on canvas, 65 x 54 cm

Hlito, Alfredo
"Volutas" 1957/58
Oil on canvas, 60 x 50 cm

Hlito, Alfredo
"Tema central" 1957
Oil on canvas, 100 x 80 cm
Private collection Switzerland

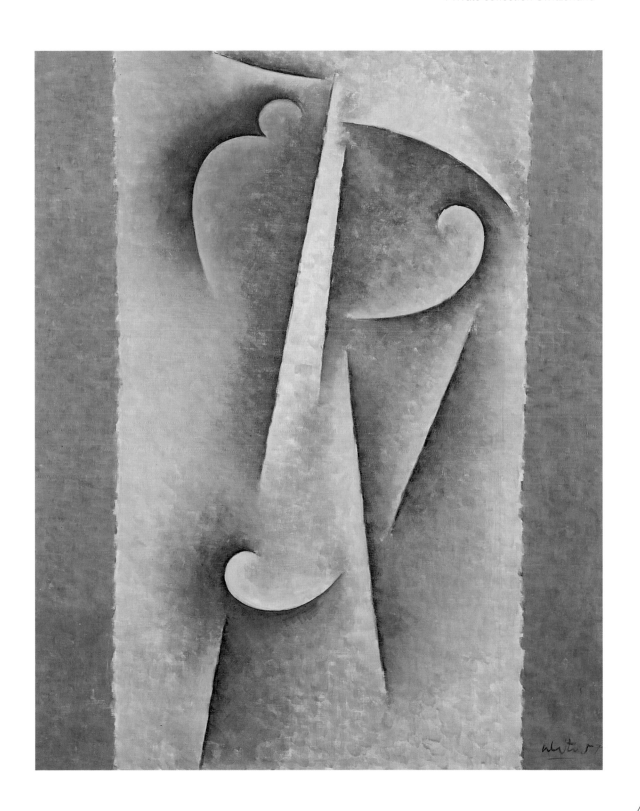

ENIO IOMMI

(b. 1926, Rosario, Argentina)

Son of an Italian sculptor with whom he first studied art; moved to Buenos Aires, 1926. Founding member of "Arte Concreto-Invención", 1945. Major exhibitions, Argentina, 1950s, including *Orientaciones actuales de la Escultura,* Galería Krayd, Buenos Aires, 1953. Gold medal, 1958 Brussels International Exposition. Showed in First Exhibition of Modern Art, Museum of Modern Art, Buenos Aires, 1960, and represented Argentina in first exhibition of *Art Concret,* Kunsthalle, Zurich, the same year. Exhibited in São Paulo Biennal, 1961. Venice Biennale, 1964, and 1st Nuremberg Biennale, 1969; retrospective, National Museum of Fine Arts, Buenos Aires, 1963. Represented in three exhibitions organized by Instituto de Tella, Buenos Aires: 1964, 1965 and 1967. Solo exhibitions at Contemporary Sculpture Centres, Tokyo and Osaka, 1987. Represented in the "Arte Concreto-Invención – Arte Madí" exhibition in Zurich 1991 and in the exhibitions of Latin American Art: "Artistas Latino-americanos del siglo XX" starting in Sevilla 1992, then in Centre Georges Pompidou, Paris 1992–1993, in Museum Ludwig, Cologne 1993 and in the Museum of Modern Art, New York 1993. Also represented in the exhibition "Argentina 1920–1994" in Museum of Modern Art, Oxford 1994. Lives and works in Buenos Aires.

Iommi, Enio
"Construcción sobre el espacio" 1946
Wood, plexiglass and metal,
43 x 56 x 62 cm

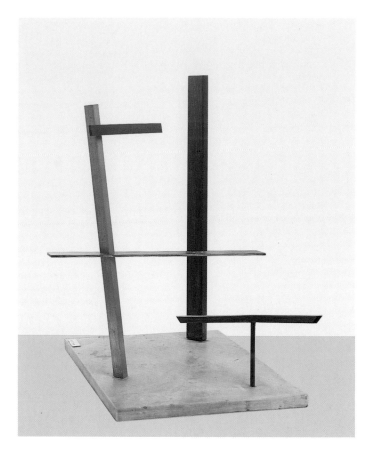

Iommi, Enio
"Construcción" 1945
Painted iron, marble, 57 cm high
Private collection Switzerland

Iommi, Enio
"Construcción" 1946
Wood, aluminium and bronze,
60 cm high
Collection E. F. Costantini, Buenos Aires

Iommi, Enio
"Direcciones espaciales" 1946
Aluminium, 49,5 cm high
Private collection Munich

Iommi, Enio
"Construcción" 1948
Bronze, 27 cm high
Private collection Basel

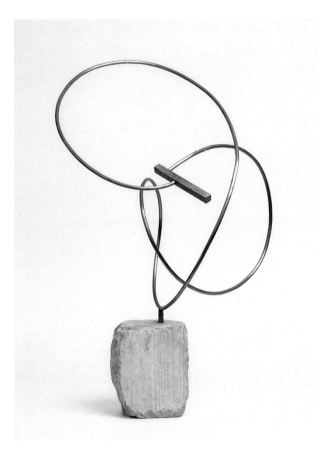

Iommi, Enio
"Continuidad" 1947
Metal and marble, 81 cm high

Iommi, Enio
"Volumen espacial" 1948
Bronze, steel and marble, 74 cm high

Iommi, Enio
"Curvas y lineas" 1948
Wood and bronze, 58 x 80 cm
Private collection Buenos Aires

Iommi, Enio
"Construcción en el espacio" 1947
Aluminium and bronze, 94 x 75,5 cm
Collection Musée de Grenoble

Iommi, Enio
"Espacialidad en los planos" 1969
Aluminium and wood, 97 cm high

Iommi, Enio
"Circulo constructivo" 1973
Aluminium, 101 cm high

Iommi, Enio
Gouache 1953, 40 x 30 cm

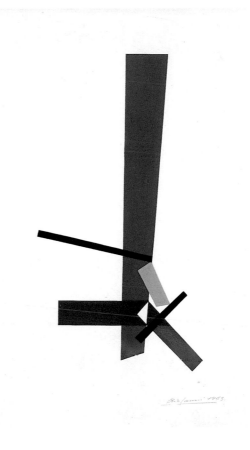

Iommi, Enio
Gouache 1953, 42 x 42 cm

GYULA KOSICE *(b. 1924, Kosice, Hungary)*

Left Hungary with his parents at age four. Studied drawing and sculpture at the Free Academy in Buenos Aires. In 1944, co-founded the review *Arturo,* succeeded by the publication *Invención.* Exhibited in *Arte Concreto-Invención,* at Dr. Pichon-Rivière's house, Buenos Aires, 1946; the same year co-founded the movement Madí and authored its manifesto. First Madí group exhibition, French Institute, Buenos Aires, 1946; founded and directed its magazine, *Arte Madí Universal,* published 1947–1954 (8 issues). Began to use plexiglas and to experiment with neon and fluorescent tubing. First solo exhibition, Pacífico Gallery, Buenos Aires, 1947; Salon des Réalités Nouvelles, Paris (1948). Settled in Paris, 1957, where he created his first hydraulic sculpture. Conceived the design for the Argentine Pavilion, 1964 Venice Biennale. Awarded International Sculpture Prize, Instituto di Tella, Buenos Aires, 1962; retrospective. Commissioned 1988 to make sculpture for Seoul Olympic Games. Represented in the "Arte Concreto-Invención – Arte Madí" exhibition in Zurich 1991 and in the exhibitions of Latin American Art: "Artistas Latino-americanos del siglo XX" in Sevilla 1992, in Centre Georges Pompidou, Paris 1992–1993, in Museum Ludwig, Cologne 1993 and in the Museum of Modern Art, New York 1993. Represented in the exhibition "Argentina 1920–1994" in Museum of Modern Art, Oxford 1994. Lives in Buenos Aires.

Kosice, Gyula
"Madi Neon No 3" 1946
Wood and neon, 56 x 41 x 18 cm
Musée de Grenoble

RAUL LOZZA

(b. 1911, Alberti, province of Buenos Aires)

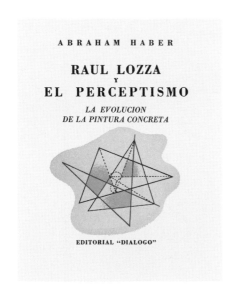

"Raúl Lozza y el Perceptismo"
Abraham Haber, Buenos Aires, 1948

During the 1930s he worked as an illustrator. By 1943 he joined the editorial board of *Contrapunto* magazine. He was a founding member of the Asociación Arte Concreto-Invención in 1945, and signed the Inventionist Manifiesto in 1946. Around 1947 he separated from the main group to create a new movement called Perceptismo, which he launched on the 31st October 1949 at the Van Riel Gallery in Buenos Aires. Published his *Manifiesto Perceptista,* which sets out the theoretical bases for the movement. In 1950, he published the first of seven issues of *Perceptismo Magazine.* In recent years he has won the Premio Palanza (1991), the Premio Konex Platino (1992) and the Premio Consagración Nacional (1992). Represented in the "Arte Concreto-Invención – Arte Madí" exhibition in Zurich 1991 and in the exhibitions of Latin American Art: "Artistas Latino-americanos del siglo XX" starting in Sevilla 1992, then in Centre Georges Pompidou, Paris 1992–1993, in Museum Ludwig, Cologne 1993 and in the Museum of Modern Art, New York 1993. Also represented in the exhibition "Argentina 1920–1994" in Museum of Modern Art, Oxford 1994. Lives and works in Buenos Aires.

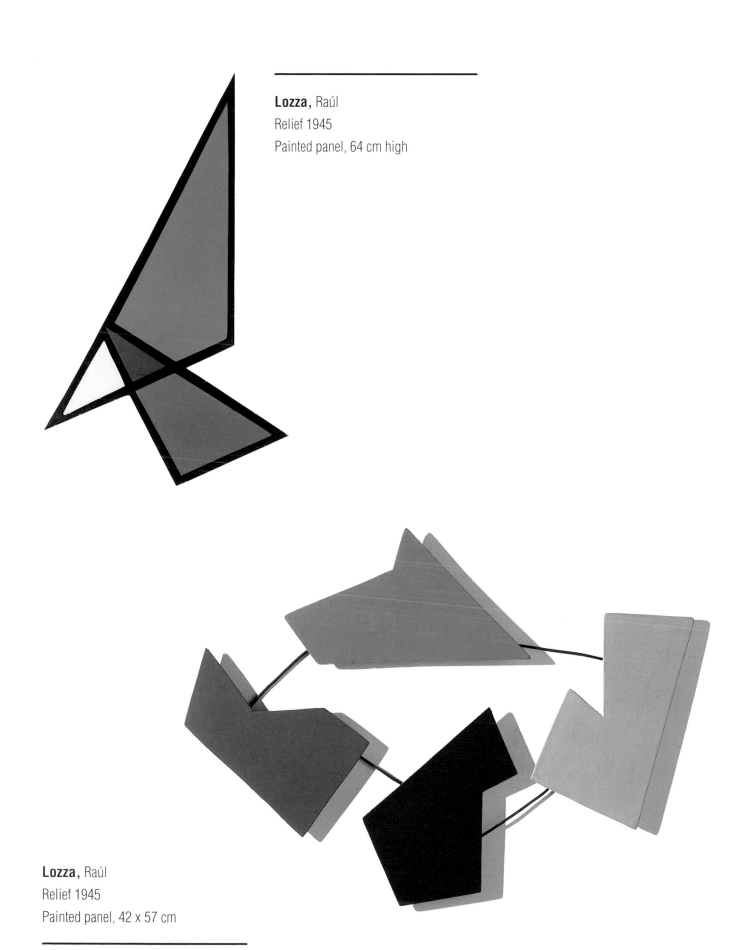

Lozza, Raúl
Relief 1945
Painted panel, 64 cm high

Lozza, Raúl
Relief 1945
Painted panel, 42 x 57 cm

Lozza, Raúl
"Pintura No 15" 1945
Oil on panel, 53,5 x 40 cm
Private collection Hamburg

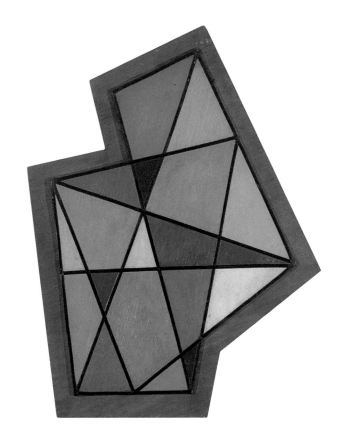

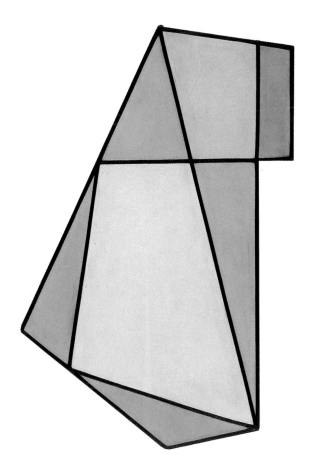

Lozza, Raúl
"Estructura analitica" 1946
Oil on panel, 52 x 32,5 cm

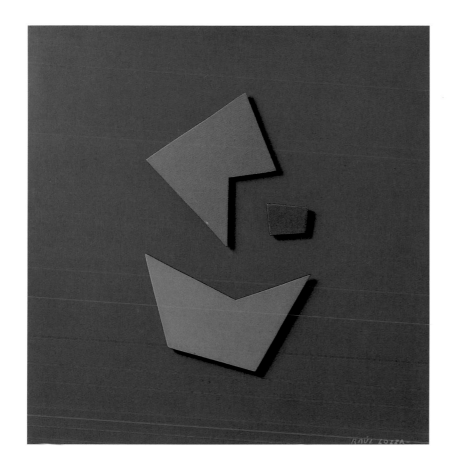

Lozza, Raúl
"Pintura No 183" 1947
Painted panel, 62 x 62 cm

Lozza, Raúl
"Invención No 150" 1948
Painted panel, 93 x 111 cm

Lozza, Raúl
"Pintura No 285" 1951
Oil on panel, 122 x 122 cm

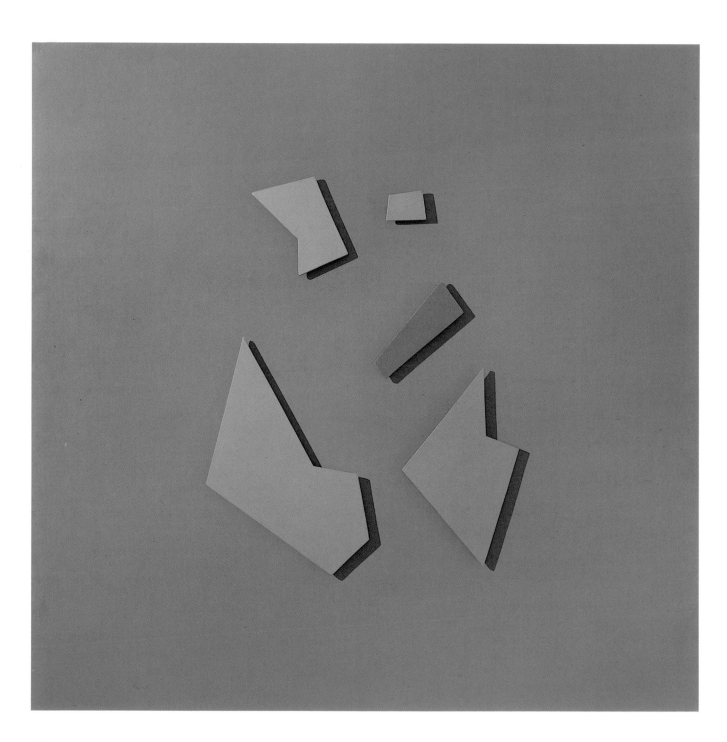

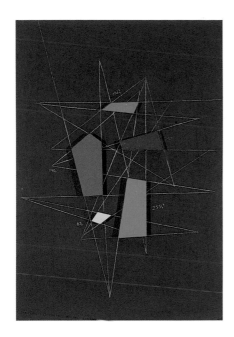

Lozza, Raúl
"Sketch to Pintura No 419" 1960
Painted panel, 60 x 40 cm
Private collection Zurich

Lozza, Raúl
"Pintura No 419" 1960
Painted panel, 122 x 94,5 cm

Tomás Maldonado and
Georges Vantongerloo, Ulm, 1955

TOMAS MALDONADO

(b. 1922, Buenos Aires)

He studied at the Academia Nacional de Bellas Artes, graduating in 1938. In 1940s he signed a manifiesto (together with Jorge Brito, Alfredo Hlito and Claudio Girola). In 1945 he separated from the *Arturo* group and, late in 1945, founded the Asociación Arte Concreto-Invención. He wrote the *Inventionist Manifiesto* with his brother, the poet Edgar Bayley, In 1948 he travelled to Europe, where he met Max Bill and Georges Vantongerloo. In 1951, with Alfredo Hlito, he was setting up the magazine *Nueva Visión*. In 1955, he left Argentina for good, invited by Max Bill to teach at the Hochschule für Gestaltung in Ulm. In 1965 he became Lethaby Lecturer at the Royal College of Art in London and, he was named Fellow of the Council of Humanities of Princeton University. In 1971 he became Professor of Environmental Planning at the University of Bologna. He has lived and worked in Italy since 1967. Represented in the "Arte Concreto-Invención – Arte Madí" exhibition in Zurich 1991 and in the exhibitions of Latin American Art: "Artistas Latino-americanos del siglo XX" starting in Sevilla 1992, then in Centre Georges Pompidou, Paris 1992–1993, in Museum Ludwig, Cologne 1993 and in the Museum of Modern Art, New York 1993. Represented in the exhibition "Argentina 1920–1994" in Museum of Modern Art, Oxford 1994.

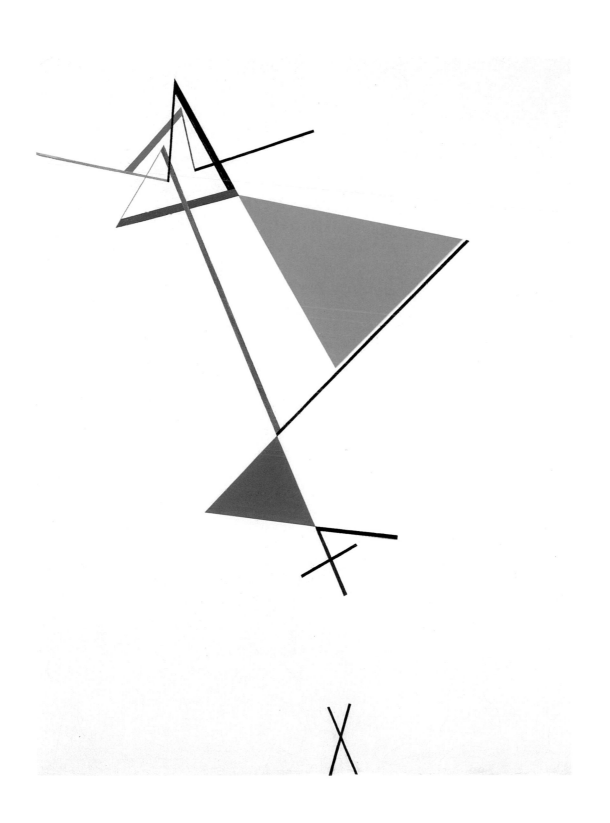

Maldonado, Tomás
"Estructura ascendente" 1949
Oil on canvas, 60 x 80 cm

Maldonado, Tomás
"Composición 208" 1951
Oil on canvas, 50 x 50 cm

Maldonado, Tomás
"Construcción de 2 elementos" 1953
Oil on canvas, 100 x 70 cm

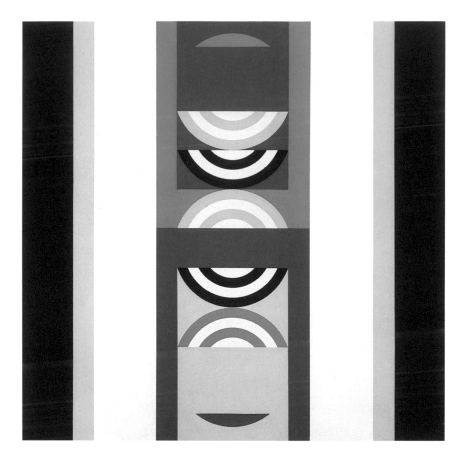

Maldonado, Tomás
"Tema central 4" 1952
Gouache on card, 80 x 80 cm

Maldonado, Tomás
"Tema central 5" 1953
Gouache on card, 80 x 80 cm

Maldonado, Tomás
"Tre zone e due temi circolari" 1953
Oil on canvas, 80 x 80 cm
Barry Friedman Ltd. New York

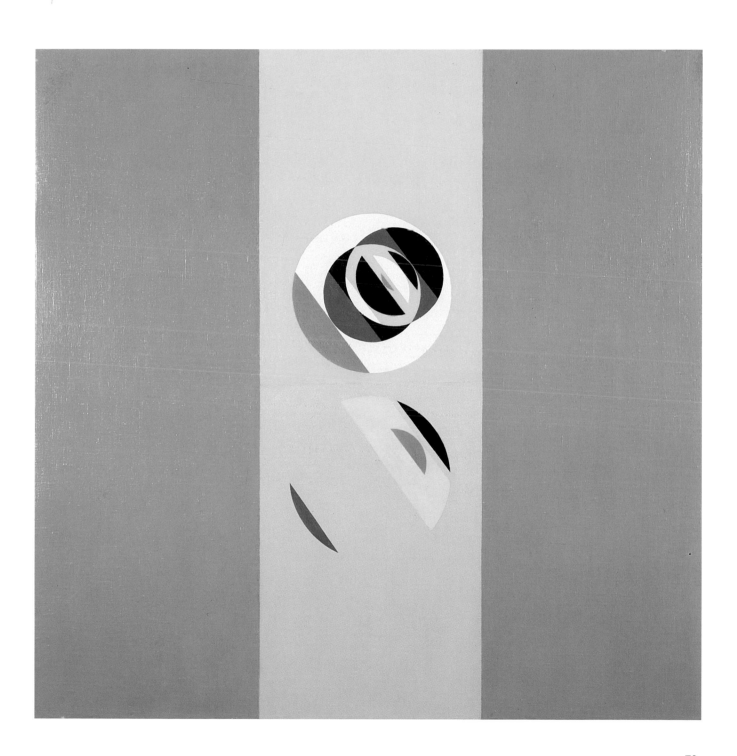

JUAN MELE

(b. 1923, Buenos Aires)

Attended National School of Fine Arts, Buenos Aires, where appointed professor of drawing, 1945. In 1946 joined "Asociación Arte Concreto-Invención", participated in group's exhibitions. To Europe to study on a French government grant; attended Ecole du Louvre, 1948, and studied privately with Vantongerloo and Sonia Delaunay; included in 1948 Salon des Réalités Nouvelles and exhibited 1949 at Maison de l'Amérique Latine, Paris. On return to Argentina, included in *Annual Exhibition of Artists under Thirty* and *Curuzú-Cuatiá* annual exhibition, both 1952; included in Il São Paulo Bienal, 1953. Exhibits regularly in Buenos Aires; has taught art and art history, and published critical articles in numerous reviews. Recent one-man exhibition in Museo de Arte Moderno, Buenos Aires (1987). Represented in the "Arte Concreto-Invención – Arte Madí" exhibition in Zurich 1991 and in the exhibitions of Latin American Art: "Artistas Latino-americanos del siglo XX" starting in Sevilla 1992, then in Centre Georges Pompidou, Paris 1992–1993, in Museum Ludwig, Cologne 1993 and in the Museum of Modern Art, New York 1993. Also represented in the exhibition "Argentina 1920–1994" in Museum of Modern Art, Oxford 1994. Lives in Buenos Aires and Paris.

Mele, Juan
"Composición" 1945
Oil on canvas, 61 x 46 cm
Private collection Basel

Mele, Juan
"Abstracción geométrica" 1945
Oil on canvas, 50 x 70 cm

Mele, Juan
"Marco recortado No 9" 1946
Painted panel, 82 x 42 cm

Mele, Juan
"Marco recortado No 10" 1946
Painted panel, 75 x 48 cm
Private collection Zurich

Mele, Juan
"Marco recortado No 2" 1946
Oil on panel, 71 x 50 cm

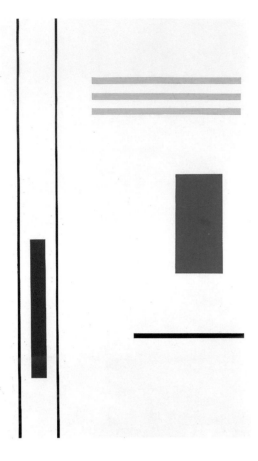

Mele, Juan
"Construcción concreta" 1946
Gouche, 74 x 45 cm
Private collection Switzerland

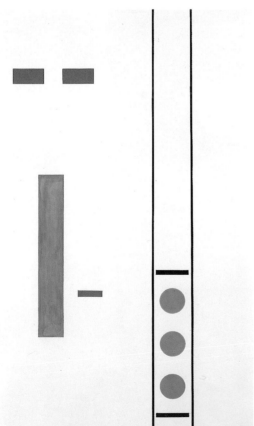

Mele, Juan
"Construcción concreta" 1946
Gouache, 74 x 45 cm
Private collection Switzerland

Mele, Juan
"Construcción concreta" 1947
Gouache, 75 x 44 cm

Mele, Juan
"Construcción concreta" 1948
Gouache, 75 x 45 cm

Mele, Juan
"Construcción concreta" 1947
Gouache, 75 x 50 cm

Mele, Juan
"Formas concretas sobre un plano"
1947
Relief, painted panel, 76 x 50 cm
Private collection U.S.A.

Mele, Juan
"Planos concretos No 35" 1948
Relief mixed media, 65 x 45 cm
Private collection

Mele, Juan
"Coplanar" 1947
Painted panel mounted on plexiglass,
87 x 110 cm

Mele, Juan
"Pintura No 36" 1954
Oil on canvas, 60 x 74 cm
Barry Friedman Ltd. New York

Mele, Juan
"Pintura No 42" 1955
Oil on panel, 80 x 60 cm

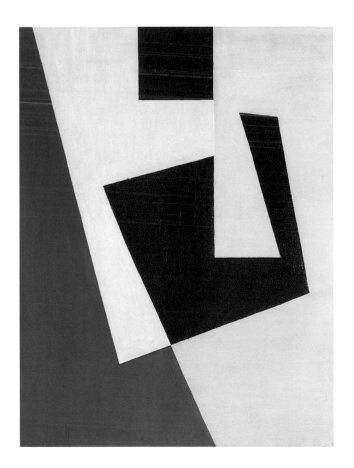

Maldonado, the brothers Lozza, Molenberg and Lidy Pratí at the occasion
of the first exhibition of "Asociación Arte
Concreto-Invención", 1946

LIDY PRATI

(b. 1921, Resistencia)

She was one of the central figures in Concrete Art in Argentina and was involved in the foundation of *Arturo* magazine in which she published several drawings (signed Lidy Maldonado). She was a founder member of the Asociación Arte Concreto-Invención. Like her husband, Tomás Maldonado, she was always interested in design and combined painting with work as a graphic designer for a number of Argentine magazines (including *Nueva Visión, Mundo argentino,* and *Artinf).* In 1952 she travelled to Europe and amongst other artists, met Max Bill, Georges Vantongerloo and Giacomo Balla. She exhibited in the 1954 São Paulo Bienal. Although she started by making paintings with irregularly shaped edges, she soon began to focus on the serial development of minimalist geometrical forms – squares or rectangles of colour, curves or monochrome lines – within a rectangular format. After stopping painting, she worked as an art critic. Represented in the "Arte Concreto-Invención – Arte Madí" exhibition in Zurich 1991 and further in the extensive series of exhibitions of Latin American Art: "Artistas Latino-americanos del siglo XX" starting in Sevilla 1992, then in Centre Georges Pompidou, Paris 1992–1993, in Museum Ludwig, Cologne 1993 and in the Museum of Modern Art, New York 1993. Lives in Buenos Aires.

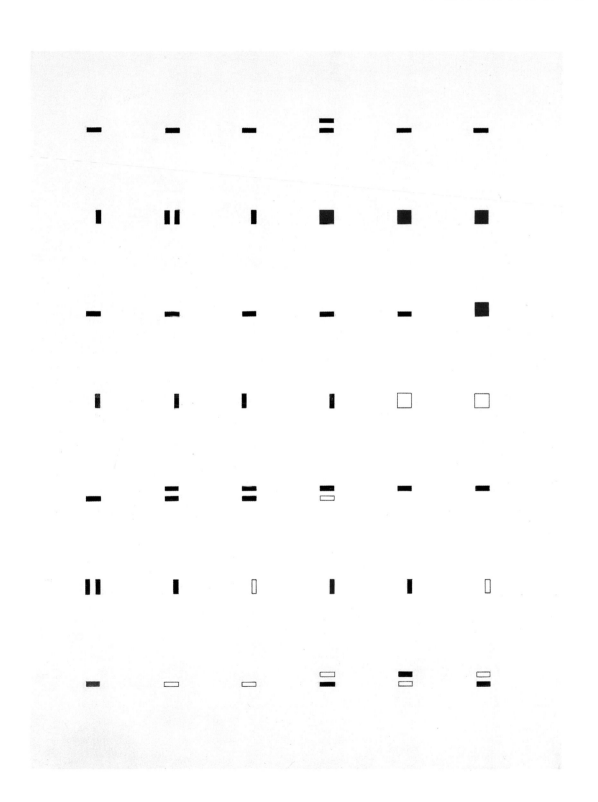

Prati, Lidy
"Concreta No 2–B" 1948
Oil on board, 60 x 60 cm
Private collection Switzerland

Prati, Lidy
without title 1951
Oil on canvas, 35 x 45 cm
Private collection Switzerland

Prati, Lidy
"Estructura vibracional" 1953
Oil on canvas, 54 x 75 cm
Private collection Zurich

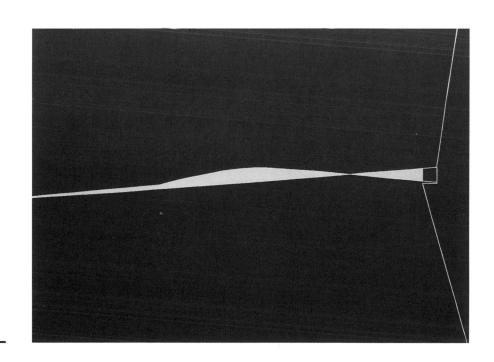

VOLF ROITMAN

(b. 1930, Montevideo, Uruguay)

In 1938 his family settled down in Buenos Aires. Studied Industrial design. Contact with the literary and plastic Avant Garde in 1950. His poems were first published in the journal "Poesía Buenos Aires". In 1951 left Argentina for Paris. Acquaintance with Arden Quin and foundation of the "Centre de Recherches et d'Etudes MADIstes". Took part in the reorganisation of the "MADI" mouvement in Paris. 1952–1956 represented at the "Réalités Nouvelles". One man show in the Galerie de Beaune in 1955 and represented at an exhibition in the Galerie Denise René in 1956. After 1956 works only as a writer. Lives and works in Barcelona.

Roitman, Volf
"Composition Madi" 1953
Lacquer on panel, 53 x 75 cm

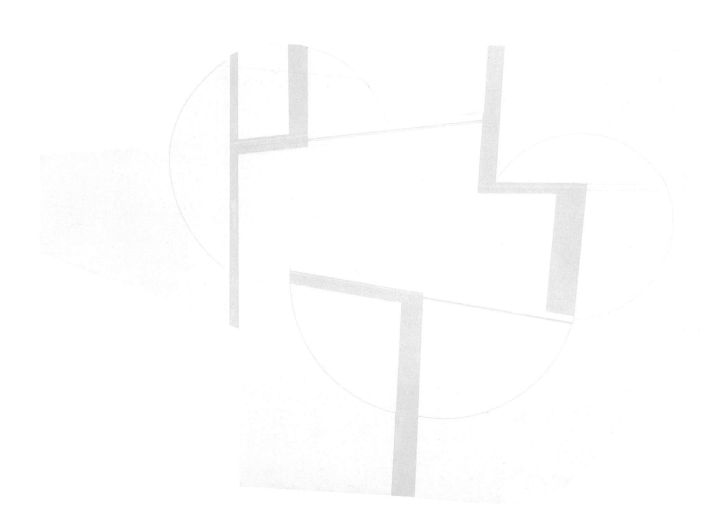

Kosice, Arden Quin and Rhod Rothfuss,
Buenos Aires, 1945

RHOD {CARLOS MARIA} ROTHFUSS

(b. 1920, Montevideo – d. 1969)

Little is known of the life of Carlos María Rothfuss, due mainly to his early death on
31st December 1969. Only a handful of his paintings and one sculpture have survived.
He studied at the Círculo de Bellas Artes in Montevideo and later became a teacher of
art. However, his most important contribution to modern art in Argentina was the article
"The frame, a problem in contemporary art" (El marco, un problema de la estética
actual), published in *Arturo* magazine in 1944. This article established the "cut frame"
as the dominant practice of the Argentine avant-garde, and predates the US invention
of the "shaped canvas" by at least a decade. Rothfuss was one of the founding members of the Madí movement in 1946, and had been one of the editors of *Arturo* two
years previously. From the late 1940s through to the 1950s, he was the official leader
of the Madí movement in Uruguay. Represented in the "Arte Concreto-Invención – Arte
Madí" exhibition in Zurich 1991 and in the exhibitions of Latin American Art: "Artistas
Latino-americanos del siglo XX" starting in Sevilla 1992, then in Centre Georges
Pompidou, Paris 1992–1993, in Museum Ludwig, Cologne 1993 and in the Museum
of Modern Art, New York 1993. Also represented in the exhibition "Argentina
1920–1994" in Museum of Modern Art, Oxford 1994.

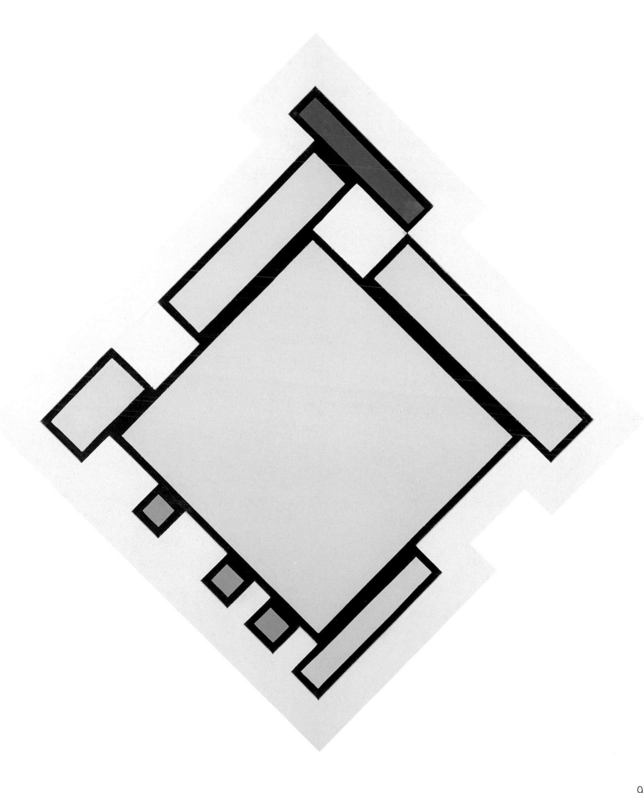

GREGORIO VARDANEGA

(b. 1923, Venice)

Moved to Argentina as a child. Studied at the Escuela Nacional de Bellas Artes. Member of the Asociación Arte Concreto-Invención from 1946. In 1948 he travelled to Paris, where he stayed until 1950. In 1955 he was a founder member of the Asociación Arte Nuevo. In 1959, he moved back to Paris. His work of the forties experimented with spatial reliefs and transparency; he also made a series of spherical sculptures in which virtual volumes were created with wires. By the late 1950s these interests had led him into the realm of Kinetic Art, using electronics, lights and reflections. Represented in the "Arte Concreto-Invención – Arte Madí" exhibition in Zurich 1991 and further in the extensive series of exhibitions of Latin American Art: "Artistas Latino-americanos del siglo XX" starting in Sevilla 1992, then in Centre Georges Pompidou, Paris 1992–1993, in Museum Ludwig, Cologne 1993 and in the Museum of Modern Art, New York 1993. Also represented in the exhibition "Argentina 1920–1994" in Museum of Modern Art, Oxford 1994. Lives and works in Paris.

Vardanega, Gregorio
Relief 1949
Wood and painted glass, 70,5 x 48 cm
Collection E. F. Costantini, Buenos Aires

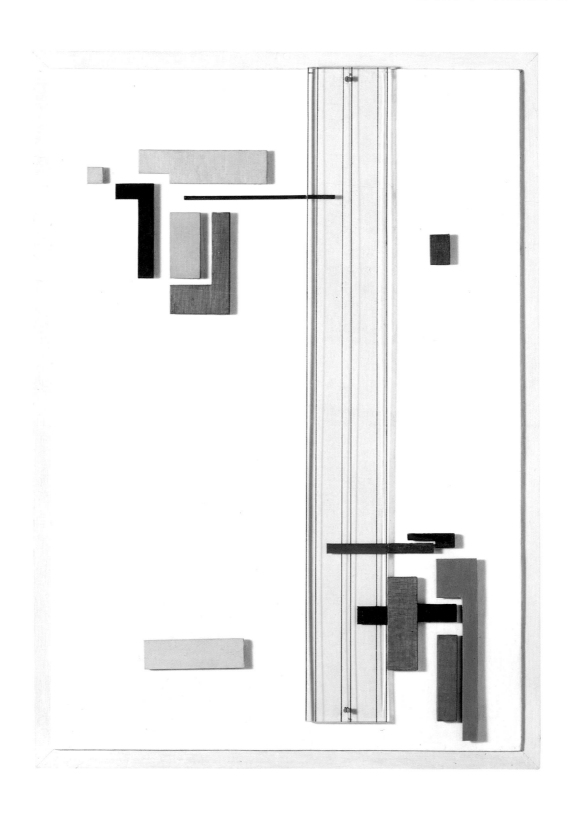

Vardanega, Gregorio
"Composition" 1948
Mixed media, 83 x 62 cm
Private collection New York

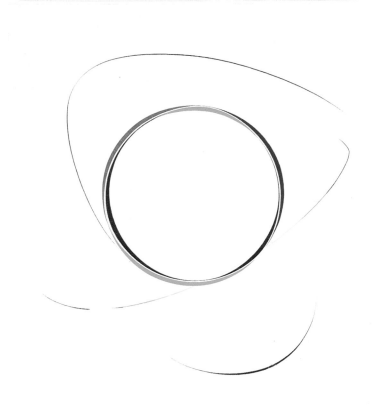

Vardanega, Gregorio
"Rotulo de identificacion" 1951
Oil on panel, 70 x 61 cm
Private collection Switzerland

Vardanega, Gregorio
"Pintura" 1953
Oil on canvas. 50 x 40 cm
Private collection Basel

Vardanega, Gregorio
"Jeu de structures" 1953
Oil on canvas, 77 x 59 cm
Private collection Basel

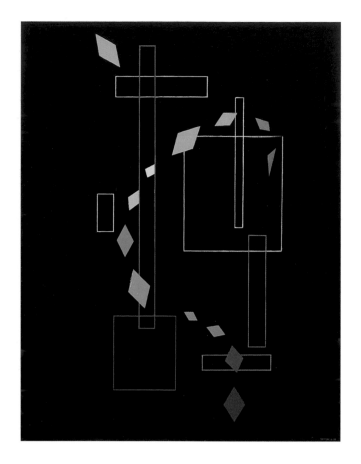

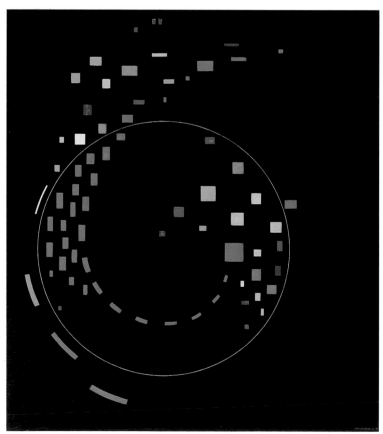

Vardanega, Gregorio
"Constelación fantasía cromatica" 1954
Oil on hardboard, 80 x 70 cm
Private collection Zurich

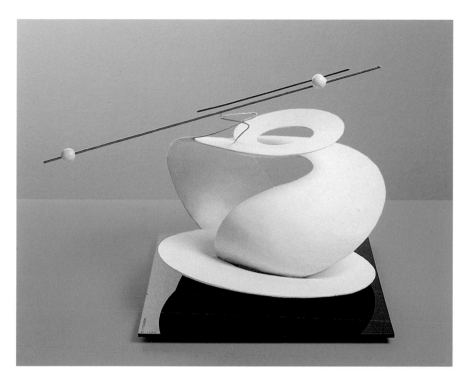

Vardanega, Gregorio
"Forme spaciale" 1954
Plaster, metal and plexiglass,
32 cm high
Private collection France

Vardanega, Gregorio
"Sagittaire" 1955/58
Oil on panel, 75 x 67 cm
Private collection Basel

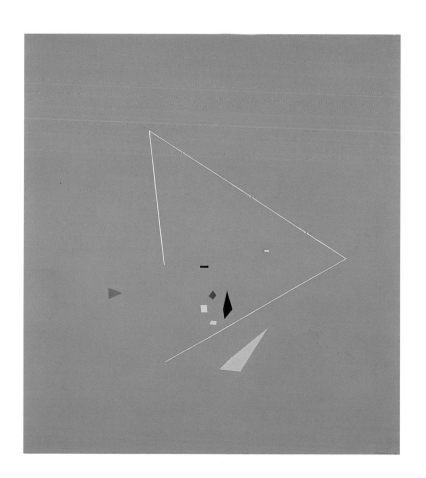

VIRGILIO VILLALBA

(b. 1925, Santa Cruz de Teneriffe, Canary Islands)

Moved to Argentina in 1929 and studied at the Escuela Nacional de Bellas Artes in Buenos Aires. He joined the Asociación Arte Concreto-Invención and took part in their exhibitions in the Galerie Kraft and Salon Peuser. 1948–1953 exhibited in the Galerie Van Riel and Salon Müller, Buenos Aires. In 1957 an article by Michel Seuphor about Villalba was published in the "Dictionnaire de la Peinture Abstraite". 1958 represented at two biennales in Mexico and Brazil. 1960 moved to Paris. 1965 exhibition in Holland and in "Artistes Latino-américains de Paris" at Musée d'Art Moderne de Paris. Represented in "Grands et Jeunes d'Aujourd'hui" in Paris 1968, 1973 and 1975. Biennale de Menton 1970, "Latino-américains de Paris" 1974 and 1982. "Argentina 1920–1994" The Museum of Modern Art, Oxford, 1994. Lives in Paris.

Villalba, Virgilio
"Horizontal composition" 1949
Oil on panel, 90,5 x 70 cm
Private collection Basel

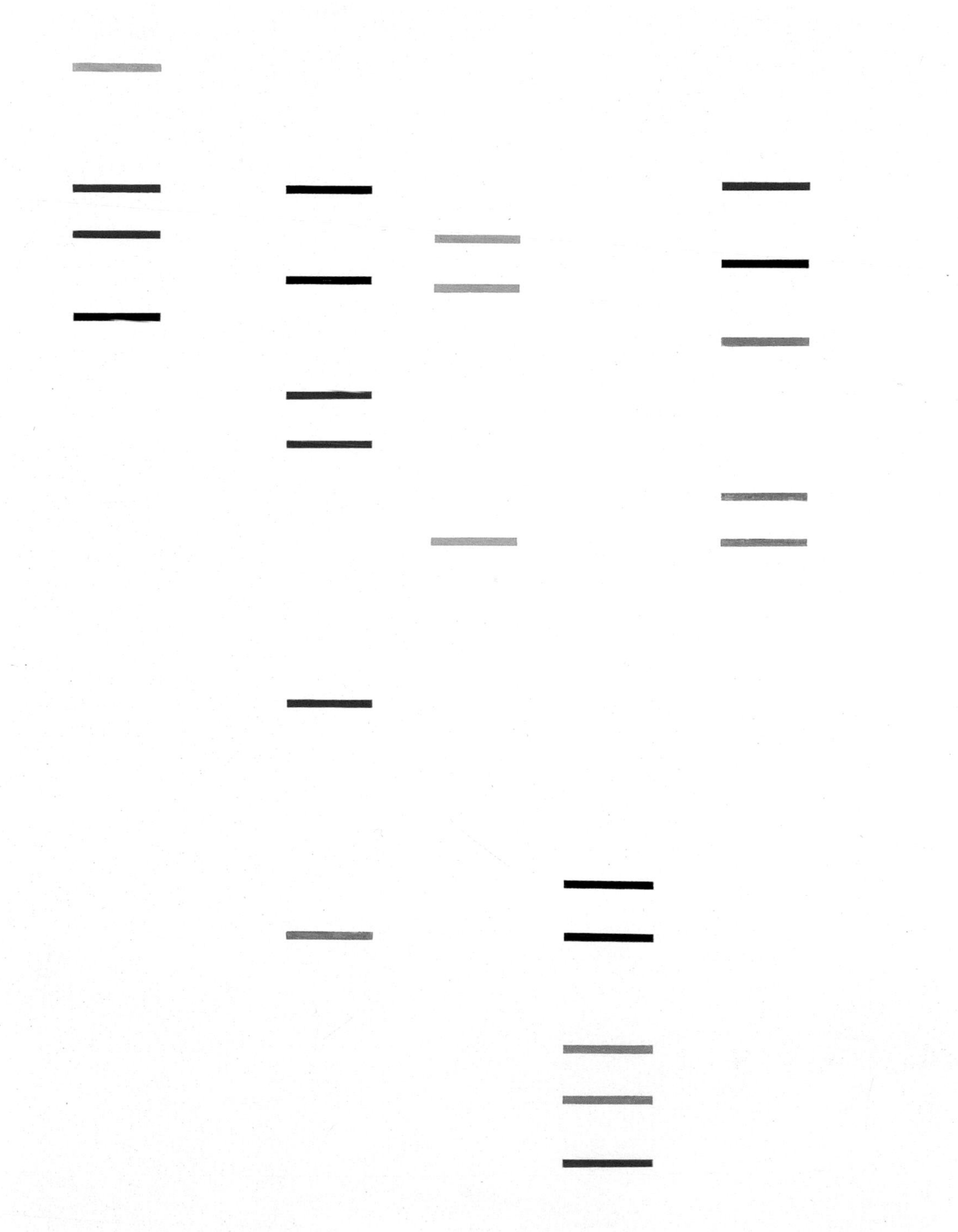

Villalba, Virgilio
"Pintura" 1949
Oil on hardboard, 49 x 49 cm
Private collection Basel

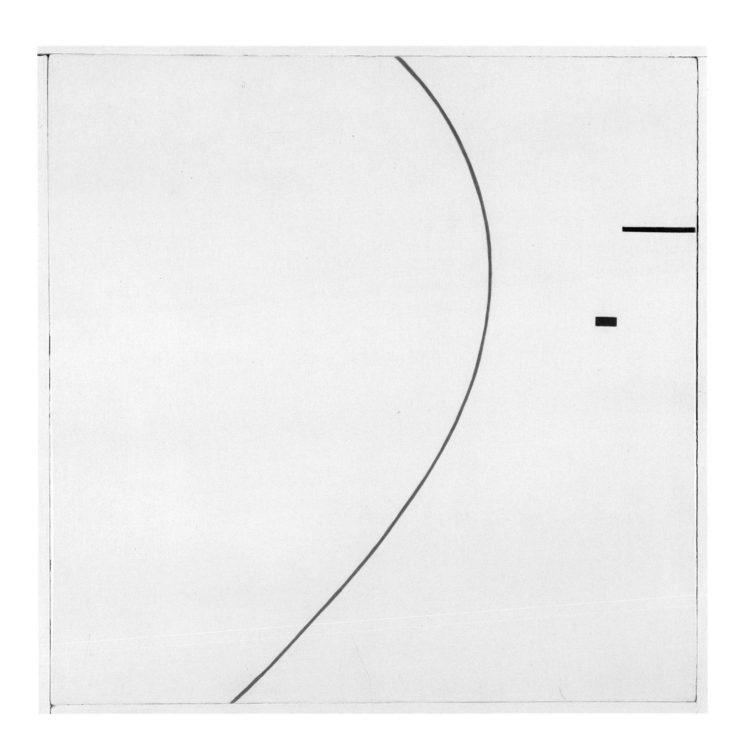

Villalba, Virgilio
without title 1957
Oil on canvas, 75 x 75 cm

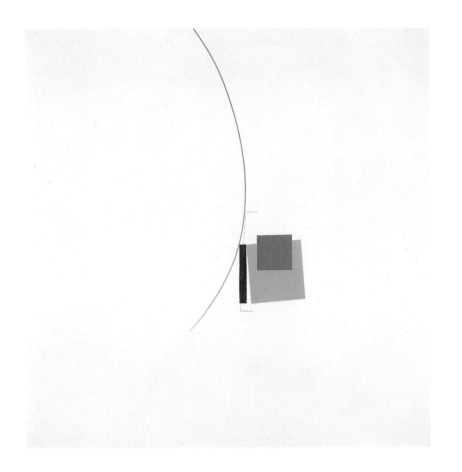

Villalba, Virgilio
without title 1957
Oil on canvas, 88 x 85 cm

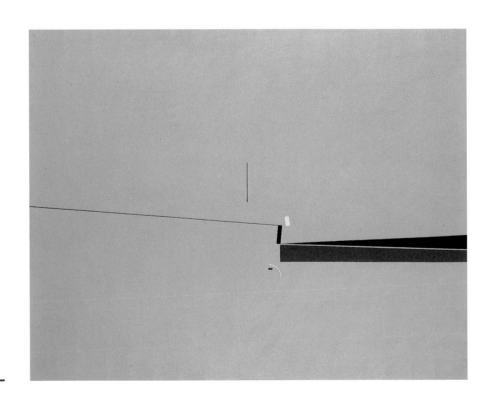

Villalba, Virgilio
without title 1957
Oil on canvas, 90 x 110 cm

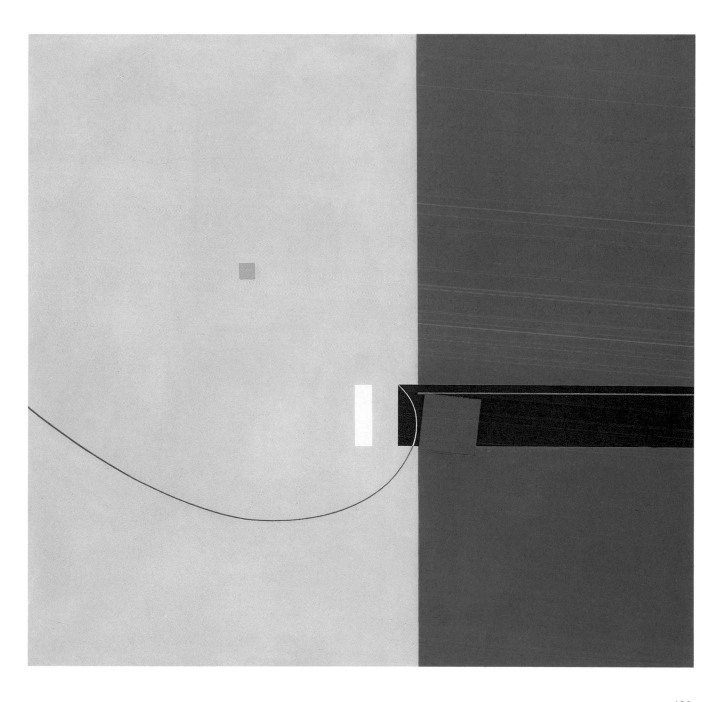

Arte Concreto Invención   Arte Madi
© 1994 Galerie von Bartha, CH-4051 Basel
Foto: Atelier Christoph Markwalder, CH-4052 Basel
Fotolitho: Fotolitho Bienna, CH-2500 Biel
Printed in Switzerland by Schudeldruck, CH-4125 Riehen